American Harvest

The American Academy of Chefs
HONOR SOCIETY OF THE AMERICAN CULINARY FEDERATION

American Harvest

Fifty Premier Chefs Share Their Favorite

Recipes from America's Regional Cuisine

Edited by Fritz Sonnenschmidt, C.M.C.
CULINARY DEAN, THE CULINARY INSTITUTE OF AMERICA

Photography by Dennis Gottlieb

LEBHAR-FRIEDMAN BOOKS
NEW YORK · CHICAGO · LOS ANGELES · LONDON · PARIS · TOKYO

For the technique photos on pages 8, 15, 46, 75, 79, 113, 125, 141, 151, and 163: Photography by Lorna Smith. Used by permission from The Culinary Institute of America from *The New Professional Chef,* 6th Edition, © 1996, published by John Wiley & Sons, Inc.

LEBHAR-FRIEDMAN BOOKS

A company of Lebhar-Friedman, Inc.

425 Park Avenue

New York, New York 10022

LIBRARY OF CONGRESS CATALOGING-IN-PUBLICATION DATA

American harvest / edited by Fritz Sonnenschmidt

      p. cm.

ISBN: 0-86730-819-2 (alk. paper)

      1. Cookery, American. I. Sonnenschmidt, Fritz.

TX715 .A50814 2000

641.5973—dc21   00-058340

ART DIRECTION: *Kevin Hanek*

FOOD STYLIST: *Elizabeth Duffy*

SENIOR MANAGING EDITOR: *Joseph Mills*

DEVELOPMENTAL EDITOR: *Justin Schwartz*

RECIPE TESTING: *Laura Pensiero*

Designed and composed by Kevin Hanek

Printed and bound by R.R. Donnelley and Sons, Roanoke, Virginia

Set in FF Scala and FF Scala Sans

Manufactured in the United States of America on acid-free paper

Visit our Web site at lfbooks.com

Contents

Soups

Sides & Salads

Poultry

Meat

Introduction

THE METAPHOR OF AMERICA AS A MELTING POT has obvious appropriateness when dealing with the subject of her cuisine. From the arrival of the earliest explorers through today, waves of people from different lands, heritages, and ethnicities have landed on these shores, melding with the existing population, and adding to the mix various aspects of their culture, and importantly, their cuisine.

Food is one of the great unifying elements of humanity. Stemming from the basic necessity of nourishing our bodies, various cultures have arrived at an astonishing number of different solutions towards fulfilling this need. As a profession, culinarians take this responsibility of nourishing the body very seriously, and it is a love for food and its restorative qualities, for both body and soul, that encourages many to pursue this course.

In *American Harvest,* the members of the American Academy of Chefs have endeavored to bring together recipes and ideas from

regions across the country. By no means intended to be an authoritative volume on American cuisine, it strives rather to offer a sampling of some of the currents running through American cuisine today. In these pages you will see cultural and ethnic influences on American cooking, to be sure, but you will also discover the ingenious manner in which Americans have shaped these influences, adapting treasured recipes and cooking techniques to the new ingredients found in their adoptive homeland, exchanging ideas with others from different backgrounds, and transforming their various culinary heritages into an indigenous American cuisine.

It is hoped that these enticing recipes, culled from across the country by some of our leading chefs, will promote a new appreciation and excitement for the evolution of America's gastronomic identity.

ABOUT THE AMERICAN CULINARY FEDERATION

Since 1929, the American Culinary Federation (ACF) has provided outstanding professional training to its members and has worked to promote a professional image of the American chef worldwide through education among culinarians at all levels. Over 10,000 certifications have been awarded by the ACF at 10 different levels ranging from Certified Culinarian to the prestigious Certified Master Chef. With a total membership of more than 25,000 members and over 300 chapters throughout the United States and the Caribbean, the ACF remains the oldest and largest organization of chefs and cooks in the United States.

ABOUT THE AMERICAN ACADEMY OF CHEFS

The American Academy of Chefs (AAC), the national honor society of chefs in America, was organized by the ACF in 1955 with the purpose of recognizing culinary professionals whose contributions have positively effected the culinary industry. Academy members have continuously practiced the highest standards and demonstrate unerringly the highest qualities of professionalism of the organization and our industry, and they support and promote education to all that follow in this profession by passing on their skills, training, and expertise.

THE SIGNIFICANCE OF THE AAC DESIGNATION

The membership of the AAC is composed of Certified Master Chefs, Certified Master Pastry Chefs, Certified Executive Chefs, Certified Executive Pastry Chefs, and Certified Culinary Educators who have earned the right to use the AAC designation by having met the criteria established by the Academy. These criteria include a minimum of 15 years in the culinary profession, 10 of which were at the executive level; ACF membership in good standing for a minimum of 10 years with certification for a minimum of 2 years; and fulfillment of 10 of the 20 mandatory requirements. The purpose of the AAC designation is to cite publicly an exceptional culinarian for professional achievements and dedication to the culinary arts as well as mentoring and community service.

THE AMERICAN ACADEMY OF CHEFS

CHAIR	Fritz Sonnenschmidt, CMC, AAC
NATIONAL VICE CHAIR	John Minniti, CCE, AAC
AMBASSADOR	Bert Cutino, CEC, AAC
CHAIR HALL OF FAME	Jon Greenwalt, CEC, AAC
VICE CHAIR CARIBBEAN REGION	Hans Schadler, CEC, AAC
VICE CHAIR CENTRAL REGION	Oliver Sommer, AAC HALL OF FAME
ASSISTANT VICE CHAIR CENTRAL REGION	John Kaufmann, CEC, AAC
VICE CHAIR HAWAIIAN REGION	Edward Frady, CEC, AAC
VICE CHAIR NORTHEAST REGION	John Schlaner, CEC, AAC
ASSISTANT VICE CHAIR NORTHEAST REGION	Gino Corelli, CEC, AAC
VICE CHAIR SOUTHEAST REGION	George Pastor, ED.D., CEC, CCE, AAC
ASSISTANT VICE CHAIR SOUTHEAST REGION	Roderick Smith, CEC, AAC
VICE CHAIR WESTERN REGION	Joseph Eidem, CEC, AAC
CHAIR PROFESSIONAL ALLIANCE AND OUTREACH COMMITTEE	John Kaufmann, CEC, AAC
CHAIR EDUCATION COMMITTEE	Thomas Macrina, CEC, AAC
CHAIR PUBLIC RELATIONS COMMITTEE	Pierre Rausch, CEC, AAC
ACADEMY ADMINISTRATOR	Kathy Scioneaux

ACKNOWLEDGMENTS

Special thanks to the following organizations for their assistance and contributions to this book:

The Culinary Institute of America

Waterford Wedgewood USA

Christofle Silver, Inc.

Lenox China

Rosenthal Chinaware USA

Bowery Kitchen Supplies, New York, NY

Ryland Inn, Whitehouse, NJ

Watershed Organic Farm, Pennington, NJ

Ort Farms, Long Valley, NJ

G & M Farms, Washington, NJ

Matarazzo Farms, North Caldwell, NJ

American Harvest

CHAPTER ONE

Soups

Soups, Chowders, and Stews

from a Variety of Heritages

S OUP IS OFTEN CITED AS THE EARLIEST PREPARED dish that prehistoric people were inspired to create. Word of this discovery must have spread quickly, as there is not a country in the world that does not have soup and its many variations as part of its cuisine.

When you look to America then, with its immigrant history, it should come as no surprise to find a rich variety of soups, stews, and chowders from around the world. Nor is it surprising that these immigrants, when recreating their native recipes, often adapted them to the new ingredients that they encountered in their adoptive homeland. The next step in the evolution of a true American cuisine occurred with the inevitable exchange of recipes and methods that resulted as people who might never have met in the Old World found themselves living and working together in the same communities.

Among the recipes in this chapter you will find both the innovative and the traditional: Sweet Potato and Butternut Squash Soup pays homage to ingredients native to the New World, while the Chanterelle Soup features a staple of Old World cuisine now cultivated on both sides of the Atlantic; Potato Soup with Sautéed Liverwurst and Pea Soup with Gravlax pair familiar dishes with unexpected flavors; and Roasted Chile Soup and Hearty Hot and Sour Soup derive from ethnic cuisine and ingredients, once considered exotic, which are now familiar components of American cooking. Inspired by the wealth of available ingredients and a variety of culinary heritages, these soups are representative of the breadth and ingenuity of America's regional cuisine.

Tomato Soup with Blood Orange and Green Peppercorns

FRITZ SONNENSCHMIDT, CMC, AAC, CULINARY DEAN,
THE CULINARY INSTITUTE OF AMERICA, HYDE PARK, NY

Christopher Columbus may have been the first Old-World inhabitant to discover the New-World tomato; it was soon introduced to Europe from Central America. At first, Spaniards and Italians called the tomato the Apple of Paradise, among other names, and were forbidden to eat it. Needless to say, the tomato became integral to modern European cooking, and Italian immigrants brought their tomato-soup recipes to America at the turn of the twentieth century. This fusion soup recipe offers a unique combination of acidities from both the tomatoes and the oranges. The green peppercorns called for in the recipe are the unripened version of the ubiquitous black peppercorns.

MAKES 4 SERVINGS

7 blood oranges (navel oranges may
    be substituted)

1 tablespoon butter

1 small onion, finely diced

2 cups vegetable broth

1 pound tomatoes, peeled and coarsely chopped

2 tablespoons ketchup

2 teaspoons green peppercorns,
    packed in brine, rinsed

1 tablespoon chopped fresh chives

Juice 5 of the oranges into a medium bowl. Using a paring knife, peel the remaining oranges, removing the outer peel and the white pith. Working over the bowl containing the orange juice, cut between the membranes, releasing the orange sections between them. Squeeze any juice from the membranes into the bowl. Place the sections in small bowl; set aside.

Heat the butter in a medium saucepan over medium heat. When it bubbles, add the onion and cook, stirring, until softened, about 5 minutes. Add the orange juice to the pan, bring to a boil, reduce the heat, and simmer, until reduced by half. Stir in the vegetable broth, tomatoes, and ketchup. Return to a boil, reduce heat to low, and simmer for 20 minutes.

Remove from the heat, stir in the green peppercorns and orange sections. Serve sprinkled with chives.

Sweet Potato and Butternut Squash Soup

KLAUS MULLER, CCE, AAC, DEAN, ACADEMY OF CULINARY ARTS,
ATLANTIC CAPE COMMUNITY COLLEGE, MAYS LANDING, NJ

This soup highlights two New World vegetables: Sweet potatoes and butternut squash are among the foods discovered by Christopher Columbus on his second voyage to what is now known as North America. In the late fifteenth century, Columbus brought them, along with many other new foods, back to Spain. There are hundreds of sweet-potato varieties. Among them is the Jersey, once the main variety grown in New Jersey. This soup underscores the natural sweetness and vibrant color of these vegetables.

MAKES 4 TO 6 SERVINGS

1 small butternut squash (about 12 ounces)

¼ cup (½ stick) butter

1 small onion, diced

¼ cup all-purpose flour

3 cups chicken stock

3 small sweet potatoes (about 12 ounces total), peeled and cubed

Pinch ground cinnamon

Pinch ground nutmeg

Pinch ground cloves

Salt and freshly ground white pepper

¼ cup heavy cream

Use a vegetable peeler to remove the skin from the butternut squash. Trim the ends, halve lengthwise, and, using a spoon, scrape out all seeds and fibers. Cut the squash halves into medium-size cubes.

Heat the butter in a medium saucepan over medium heat. Add the onion and cook, stirring, until translucent, about 5 minutes. Sprinkle the flour into the pan and stir to evenly incorporate with the butter to form a roux. Cook, stirring, for 2 to 3 minutes. Add the chicken stock, squash, sweet potatoes, and spices, and season with salt and pepper. Bring to a boil, lower the heat, and simmer, until the squash and potatoes can easily be pierced with a sharp knife, about 20 minutes. Add the cream and cook another 1 to 2 minutes, then remove the soup from the heat.

Puree the soup, using a hand-held blender or a food processor, in batches if necessary, until smooth. Adjust the seasonings and serve. If the consistency is too thick, thin with a little more hot stock. The thickness of the soup can vary greatly, depending on how quickly the soup has been simmered and, although the soup should be thick, you may need to add up to a cup of stock to achieve the desired texture.

Chanterelle Soup

WILLI DAFFINGER, CEC, AAC, EXECUTIVE CHEF,
ROLLING ROCK CLUB, LIGONIER, PA

My mother made this soup often. I grew up in Bavaria, a very woodsy country where mushrooms grow wild. Western Pennsylvania, where I live and work now, has a similar landscape. Wild mushrooms are commonly available here, including morels, harvested in the spring and beautiful chanterelles, found in the summer.

MAKES 4 TO 6 SERVINGS

½ cup diced uncooked slab bacon

½ cup minced shallots

2 cups sliced chanterelle mushrooms

½ cup dry white wine, such as Sauvignon Blanc

3 tablespoons all-purpose flour

3 cups hot chicken stock

½ teaspoon freshly grated lemon zest

Pinch caraway seeds

Salt and freshly ground black pepper

½ cup heavy cream

1 teaspoon chopped flat-leaf parsley

In a medium saucepan, cook the bacon over medium heat, stirring, until it just begins to brown, 3 to 4 minutes. Add the shallots, reduce the heat to low, and cook, stirring often, until they are soft and glazed, 2 to 3 minutes.

Add the chanterelles, increase the heat to medium-high, and cook, stirring, for another 2 minutes. Add the wine. Simmer until the wine is reduced by half, then add the flour and cook, stirring, for 1 to 2 minutes. Slowly pour in the chicken stock, stirring to prevent lumps, and bring to a boil. Simmer for 30 minutes. Add the lemon zest, caraway seeds, and salt and pepper, and cook another 5 minutes. Add the heavy cream, stir to blend, and return to a simmer. Remove the pan from the heat. Stir in the parsley and serve.

MAKING CHICKEN STOCK

A basic chicken stock can be used as the basis for many different soups and sauces. The same procedure is followed when making stock from veal, beef, or fish. For every gallon of stock, you will need 8 pounds of bones and trimmings, 6 quarts of water, 1 pound of *mirepoix* (chopped aromatic vegetables, usually onion, carrot, and celery), and a *bouquet garni* (see page 26).

Be sure to assemble all the ingredients before starting, and be sure to clean all work surfaces and utensils thoroughly before and after handling poultry. The method for making chicken stock is as follows:

1. Combine the bones with enough cold water to cover them, and bring the water slowly to a boil over low heat (Fig. 1).

2. Skim the surface to remove any impurities that arise during cooking (Fig. 2).

3. Once the stock is clear of impurities, bring it to a simmer (Fig. 3). The stock should be allowed to simmer between 3 and 5 hours for the best flavor.

4. Add the *mirepoix*, or combination of chopped aromatic vegetables such as onion, carrot, and celery, to the stock (Fig. 4). Ideally this should be added in the last hour of cooking. The stock will lose some volume as it cooks.

5. Ladle the finished stock through a cheesecloth to strain it (Fig. 5). Be careful to disturb the bones as little as possible to retain the stock's clarity.

6. Cool the strained stock in an ice water bath (Fig. 6). The stock should be cooled to around 40°F, at which point it can be transferred to storage containers.

1.

2.

3.

4.

5.

6.

Pea Soup with Gravlax

FRITZ SONNENSCHMIDT, CMC, AAC, CULINARY DEAN,
THE CULINARY INSTITUTE OF AMERICA, HYDE PARK, NY

French settlers may have brought their recipes for pea soup to America, but it has become a true product of the American heartland—a satisfying dish that can help sustain a farm family through winter hardship. Though adding gravlax is my own variation, this recipe is an American melting pot of French and Scandinavian cultures; it's a unique example of how the harvest of the land and the bounty of the sea can be combined in new and creative ways. We've provided a recipe for making gravlax, but any smoked salmon may be substituted.

MAKES 6 SERVINGS

2 tablespoons olive oil

2 shallots, finely diced

1 pound dry split peas

6 cups chicken broth

1 medium potato, peeled and diced

$^1/_2$ cup sour cream

$^1/_2$ cup heavy cream

Salt and freshly ground black pepper

Six 1-ounce pieces gravlax (recipe follows)

6 mint leaves

FOR THE GRAVLAX:

2 tablespoons olive oil

Juice of 2 lemons

2 tablespoons brandy (optional)

$2^1/_2$ cups white or brown sugar

$^3/_4$ cup kosher salt

$^1/_3$ cup black or white peppercorns

2 bunches fresh dill, coarsely chopped

2 salmon fillets ($1^1/_2$ to 2 pounds each),
   cleaned, skin on

Heat the olive oil in a medium saucepan set over medium heat. Add the shallots and cook, stirring, 2 to 3 minutes. Add the split peas and toast them for 2 minutes, stirring continuously to prevent sticking or burning.

Pour the broth into the pan; add the potato. Bring to a boil, then lower the heat, partially cover, and cook at a simmer, stirring often, until the peas are cooked, about 45 minutes. Using a hand-held blender, or in a food processor or blender, puree the soup in batches if necessary. Add the sour cream and the cream, return the soup to a boil, and season with salt and pepper. Ladle into soup bowls, lay a slice of gravlax in the center, and top with a mint leaf.

TO MAKE GRAVLAX:

In a small bowl, combine the olive oil, lemon juice, and brandy, if using. In a medium bowl, toss the sugar, salt, peppercorns, and dill.

Brush the olive oil and lemon juice mixture over the salmon fillets, being sure to use all of it. Then pack the sugar and salt mixture evenly over both sides of the fillets. Tightly wrap the coated fillets in plastic wrap, lay them flat in a roasting pan, and place something that weighs a few pounds on top, such as a cast-iron skillet. Refrigerate for 2 to 3 days.

When ready to serve, scrape the marinade from the salmon and thinly slice on the bias, leaving the skin behind.

This recipe for gravlax makes much more than you'll need for the pea soup recipe. You can serve the leftovers in a variety of ways, such as for breakfast with scrambled eggs, or with bagels and cream cheese. It will last in the refrigerator for 3 to 4 days, or can be stored in a resealable plastic bag in the freezer for about a month.

Potato Soup with Sautéed Liverwurst

FRITZ SONNENSCHMIDT, CMC, AAC, CULINARY DEAN,
THE CULINARY INSTITUTE OF AMERICA, HYDE PARK, NY

In the late nineteenth century, German settlers made their way to the American Northwest, including Idaho. Although that state is now famous for its potatoes, German immigrants brought their recipe for hearty potato soup from their homeland. Though liverwurst or other sausage would traditionally have been served on the side, I tried adding the liverwurst to the soup. The combination of flavors is excellent. The Braunschweiger liverwurst called for in the recipe is hard, unlike the more common soft variety, and can be found in most supermarkets.

MAKES 6 TO 8 SERVINGS

4 tablespoons butter

3 shallots, minced

1 celery stalk, chopped

½ carrot, peeled and diced

½ leek, rinsed well, white and light green parts, thinly sliced

6 cups chicken broth

1 pound starchy potatoes (such as russet), peeled and cut into 2-inch cubes

2 marjoram leaves, finely chopped, or ½ teaspoon dried

Pinch ground nutmeg

Salt and freshly ground black pepper

Eight 1-ounce slices of hard Braunschweiger liverwurst

4-5 tablespoons whipped cream, for serving

Melt 3 tablespoons of the butter in a large saucepan over medium heat. Add the shallots and cook, stirring, until translucent, 2 to 3 minutes. Add the celery, carrot, and leek, and cook, stirring often, until they are slightly softened, about 5 minutes.

Add the chicken broth and potatoes. Increase the heat to bring the mixture to a boil. Reduce the heat and simmer, until the vegetables are tender, about 25 minutes. Season with marjoram, nutmeg, and salt and pepper.

While the soup cooks, heat the remaining tablespoon of butter in a large non-stick skillet over medium-high heat. When the butter bubbles, add the liverwurst to the pan and cook until lightly browned on both sides, 1 to 2 minutes per side. Place a teaspoon or two of the whipped cream atop each serving of soup, and place a slice of liverwurst in the center of the whipped cream.

Roasted Chile Soup

VICTOR A. L. GIELISSE, CMC, CHE, ASSOCIATE VICE PRESIDENT AND DEAN OF CULINARY, BAKING AND PASTRY STUDIES, THE CULINARY INSTITUTE OF AMERICA, HYDE PARK, NY

Gone are the days when chiles were considered purely southwestern fare. Nowadays, exotic chiles are used in all types of cuisine. In this soup, the smokiness and mild heat of the chipotles and poblanos balances the sweetness of the bell peppers.

MAKES 4 TO 6 SERVINGS

6 green bell peppers

4 red bell peppers

4 poblano peppers

3 tablespoons olive oil

1 large onion, diced

5 cloves garlic, minced

2 medium tomatoes, peeled (see note), seeded, and diced

1/4 cup chopped chipotle chiles (canned, packed in adobo sauce)

1 teaspoon ground cumin

1 quart chicken stock

1 cup heavy cream

Salt and freshly ground black pepper

Preheat the oven to 500°F.

To roast and peel the bell peppers, lightly rub the peppers with 1 tablespoon of olive oil and arrange them in an even layer in a large roasting pan. Place the pan in the oven and roast, frequently shaking the pan or turning the peppers using kitchen tongs, until the peppers collapse, about 30 minutes. Transfer the roasted peppers to a large bowl and cover tightly with plastic wrap. When cool enough to handle, remove the skin, seeds, and stems. Dice and set aside.

In a medium saucepan, heat the remaining 2 tablespoons of olive oil over medium heat. Add the onion and garlic and cook, stirring, until translucent, about 5 minutes. Stir in the diced tomatoes, chipotles, and cumin. Add the roasted peppers and chicken stock, and bring to a boil. Reduce heat, simmer for 20 minutes.

Stir the heavy cream into the saucepan, bring to a boil, then remove from the heat. Using a hand-held blender, or a food processor or blender, puree the mixture, in batches if necessary, until the consistency is smooth. Season with salt and pepper and serve.

TO PEEL TOMATOES:

Carefully submerge the tomatoes in a large pot of boiling water. After about 45 seconds, remove with a slotted spoon and plunge into ice water to stop cooking. The skins will easily peel off.

Curried Ginger-Pumpkin Bisque

HANS J. SCHADLER, CEC, AAC, EXECUTIVE CHEF,
CANEEL BAY RESORT, ST. JOHN, U.S. VIRGIN ISLANDS

West Indian pumpkin, curry, and ginger are integral ingredients in Caribbean cooking. This soup combines the sweet-and-spicy contrasts found in U.S. Virgin Islands cooking.

MAKES 4 TO 6 SERVINGS

2 pounds West Indian pumpkin (*calabaza*),
    or sugar pumpkin or acorn squash

2 tablespoons butter

1 onion, diced

1 teaspoon minced fresh ginger

1 lemon grass stalk, peeled and finely minced

2 cloves garlic, minced

1 Granny Smith apple, peeled, cored, and diced

1 carrot, peeled and diced

2 teaspoons curry powder

Pinch turmeric

1 teaspoon chopped fresh thyme,
    or 1/2 teaspoon dried

1/4 cup coconut milk

1 teaspoon light brown sugar

1 quart chicken stock or vegetable stock

1 bay leaf

1/3 cinnamon stick

2 whole cloves

2 teaspoons vegetable oil

2 cups heavy cream

Salt, freshly ground black pepper,
    and cayenne pepper

Preheat the oven to 350°F.

Using a large knife, cut the pumpkin in half or into wedges. Scoop out the strings and discard; reserve the seeds. Using a paring knife, peel each piece, then cut the flesh into medium chunks. Set aside.

In a large saucepan, melt the butter over medium-high heat. Add the onion and cook, stirring often, until softened, about 5 minutes. Add the ginger, lemon grass, and garlic. Cook, stirring constantly, until aromatic, about 30 seconds, then add the pumpkin, apple, and carrot. Cook, stirring, 2 to 3 minutes. Add the curry, turmeric, and thyme. After 1 minute, add the coconut milk and brown sugar; cook 1 minute more.

Pour the chicken or vegetable stock into the saucepan; bring to a boil. While the soup heats, place the bay leaf, cinnamon stick, and cloves in a small piece of cheesecloth and tie securely closed. Add to the saucepan. After the soup boils, reduce the heat, and simmer for 30 minutes, or until all vegetables are very soft.

Meanwhile, remove any remaining strings from the pumpkin seeds and rinse the seeds in a large bowl of water. Strain and pat dry between sheets of paper towel. In a medium bowl, toss the seeds with the vegetable oil to coat evenly. Spread in an even layer on a small baking sheet and bake in the preheated oven, tossing or stirring occasionally, until lightly browned and crisp, about 25 minutes. Set aside.

Remove the cheesecloth bundle from the soup and discard. Using a hand-held blender directly in the saucepan, or in a food processor or blender, puree until smooth, in batches if necessary. Stir in the heavy cream and heat until almost boiling. Remove the soup from the heat and season with the salt, black pepper, and cayenne pepper. Garnish with the toasted pumpkin seeds.

Pot of Fire

S. B. "DOC" JENSEN, CEC, CCE, AAC, FORMER PROFESSOR EMERITUS,
ADIRONDACK COMMUNITY COLLEGE, QUEENSBURY, NY

Rooted in the farm communities' tradition of sharing the harvest, versions of this recipe can be found throughout the world. Historically, the fall harvest was so busy that little time was left for cooking. Thus, a host would supply the meat, and other farmers would bring such vegetables as cabbage, carrots, potatoes, and turnips. Everyone would contribute to preparation and, in the end, a hearty soup was prepared and shared. In the American South, where this dish is called *corn pone* and *pot liquor,* adults enjoy the meat and vegetables and children receive the broth and fresh baked corn bread.

MAKES 4 SERVINGS

2 tablespoons peanut oil

4 skinless, boneless chicken breasts
    (about 6 ounces each)

Salt and freshly ground black pepper

2 tablespoons clarified butter
    (see technique on facing page)

1 large onion, sliced

2 tablespoons minced fresh garlic

1 quart chicken stock

4 medium russet potatoes, peeled and quartered

4 medium turnips, peeled and cut into
    ¹/₂-inch cubes

4 baby carrots, peeled (leave ¹/₂-inch stem on)

Pinch saffron

8 snow pea pods, sliced lengthwise into thin strips

In a large saucepan, heat the peanut oil over medium-high heat. Season the chicken breasts with salt and pepper and add them to the pan. Cook 3 to 4 minutes per side, or until well browned, then transfer to a plate and set aside.

Add the clarified butter to the pan along with the onion and garlic. Cook, stirring, for 2 to 3 minutes, then add the chicken, chicken stock, potatoes, turnips, baby carrots, and saffron. Bring to a boil, then reduce the heat and simmer until the vegetables are tender, about 25 minutes. Season with salt and pepper. Garnish with the snow peas.

CLARIFYING BUTTER

The purpose of clarifying butter is to be able to cook with butter at a higher temperature than would be possible with whole butter. The milk solids in whole butter scorch easily and lower its smoking point.

Because it has some butter flavor, clarified butter is often used for sautéing, sometimes in combination with a vegetable oil to further raise the smoking point. It is also commonly used to make a roux. The process of clarifying butter is as follows:

1. Melt the butter in a heavy saucepan over moderate heat. Continue to cook over low heat until the butter becomes very clear and the milk solids drop to the bottom of the pot. Skim the surface foam (Fig. 1) as the butter clarifies.

2. Pour or ladle the clarified butter from the saucepan into another container (Fig. 2), being careful to leave the milk solids (Fig. 3) behind. Discard the remaining solids.

3. Figure 4 shows butter in its various stages: just melted (left), butter beginning to clarify (center), and fully clarified butter (right).

1.

2.

3.

4.

Hearty Hot and Sour Soup

MARTIN YAN, AAC, YAN CAN COOK, INC.

No matter where you travel, if you can find a Chinese restaurant, you can find hot-and-sour soup. I wouldn't have it any other way, as this soothing soup, with its pleasing balance of tartness and piquancy, is one of my favorites. Now, you can make it at home to have on hand for whenever you need a steaming bowl of Chinese comfort.

MAKES 6 TO 8 SERVINGS

6 cups chicken broth

$^1/_4$ pound boneless pork, thinly sliced

6 shiitake mushrooms, stems discarded, caps thinly sliced

$^1/_2$ cup sliced bamboo shoots, fresh or canned

6 tablespoons Chinese rice vinegar

2 ounces cooked small shrimp

$^1/_4$ cup frozen peas, thawed

$^1/_4$ cup soy sauce

2 teaspoons sesame oil

$^3/_4$ teaspoon freshly ground white pepper

3 tablespoons cornstarch, dissolved in $^1/_4$ cup water

1 large egg, lightly beaten

1 tablespoon chopped fresh cilantro

Heat the broth in a large saucepan over medium-high heat. Bring to a boil, add the pork, mushrooms, and bamboo shoots. Reduce the heat to low, and simmer, stirring occasionally, for 3 minutes.

Add the vinegar, shrimp, peas, soy sauce, sesame oil, and white pepper. Stir to combine, simmer for 3 minutes; add the cornstarch mixture. Cook, stirring, until the soup thickens, 2 to 3 minutes. Remove from the heat, add the egg, stirring constantly, until long threads form. Divide the soup among serving bowls and sprinkle with the cilantro.

Trotten Inlet Oyster Stew

JIM WOLTERS, CEC, AAC, MANITO COUNTRY CLUB, SPOKANE, WA

Many coastal areas have their own version of oyster stew. The local ingredients of Washington State make this a particularly special one. Trotten Inlet is located just north of Olympia, in the south Puget Sound. In the algae-rich waters, oysters grow quickly and have an intense, rich flavor. Combined with the fresh, young asparagus from Walla Walla, they make a unique oyster stew.

MAKES 4 SERVINGS

20 Trotten Inlet oysters (other oysters, around 1½ inches long, may be substituted)

8 ounces Walla Walla asparagus (or substitute local asparagus)

1 tablespoon butter

2 scallions, thinly sliced

2 tablespoons finely diced red bell pepper

1 quart heavy cream

1 teaspoon dry mustard

1 teaspoon Worcestershire sauce

¼ teaspoon ground white pepper

Salt

2 tablespoons chopped flat-leaf parsley

Fill a large pot three-quarters full of water, bring to a boil, then generously salt. Fill a large bowl with ice water and set aside.

Scrub the shells of the oysters. Using an oyster knife, working over a bowl to capture their liquor, shuck the oysters.

Snap off the ends of the asparagus, then, using a peeler, peel the stems. Place the asparagus spears in the boiling water, and cook until just tender, about 3 minutes. Drain. Transfer the asparagus to an ice-water bath to quickly stop cooking. Drain again. Cut the asparagus spears into ¼-inch-thick slices on the bias. Set aside.

Melt the butter in a medium saucepan over medium heat. Add the scallions and bell pepper and cook, stirring, 2 to 3 minutes. Add the cream, the oysters and their liquor, dry mustard, and Worcestershire sauce, and season with the white pepper and salt to taste. Bring to a boil, reduce the heat, and simmer for 5 minutes, poaching the oysters. Add the asparagus and simmer for 3 minutes.

Stir in the parsley and ladle the stew into bowls, allotting 5 oysters to each.

Billi Bi
(Mussel Soup)

MARC H. VEDRINES, CEC, AAC, FORMER OWNER,
THE FRENCH POODLE RESTAURANT, CARMEL, CA

During the late sixties and early seventies, I was the executive chef at The Lodge in Pebble Beach. At that time, mussels could be plucked from the rocks of the seventh and seventeenth holes of the golf course, which bordered a still-water cove. These mussels can no longer be found, but those grown on aquatic farms are available in markets year round.

MAKES 6 SERVINGS

3 cups heavy cream

2 cups Meursault or Chablis wine

2 shallots, diced

1 small onion, diced

18 mussels, well scrubbed

Salt and cayenne pepper

1 bunch chives, finely chopped

In a large saucepan, over medium heat bring the cream, wine, shallots, and onion to a boil. Reduce the heat to maintain a low boil, add the mussels, and cook, partially covered, 10 minutes, or until the mussels have opened. Season to taste with salt and cayenne pepper. Strain the soup and divide among the serving bowls. Place 2 to 3 mussels in each bowl and sprinkle with the chives.

Corn and Lobster Chowder

GERALD P. BONSEY, CEC, AAC, EXECUTIVE CHEF,
THE YORK HARBOR INN, YORK HARBOR, ME

For more than fifty years, Rockland, Maine has hosted the Annual Maine Lobster Festival every August. About eight tons of lobster are consumed at this multiday event overlooking Penobscot Bay, which draws up to 75,000 attendees from around the country and the world. Live music performances, coronations, a parade, and unlimited seafood await visitors. Wait until the weather turns cool before trying my recipe for warm and satisfying lobster chowder, an interpretation of a New England classic.

MAKES 4 SERVINGS

3 tablespoons butter

1/3 cup diced onion

1/3 cup diced celery

1 1/2 cups fresh corn kernels, cut from the cob
(frozen corn may be substituted)

1/4 cup all-purpose flour

1 cup chicken stock

8 ounces fresh Maine lobster meat, diced

2 small red potatoes, diced

3/4 cup heavy cream

1/4 cup diced red bell pepper

1/4 cup diced green bell pepper

1/4 teaspoon dried thyme

1 bay leaf

Salt and freshly ground white pepper

In a medium saucepan, heat the butter over medium heat. When melted, add the onion, celery, and corn, and cook, stirring, 5 minutes. Sprinkle with flour, and cook, stirring, 1 minute. Add the chicken stock, stirring to blend, and bring to a boil. Reduce the heat to low, and simmer 15 minutes. Add the lobster, potatoes, cream, red and green peppers, thyme, and bay leaf; season with salt and pepper. Simmer, stirring occasionally, until the potatoes are cooked, about 10 minutes.

Confederate Corn and Crab Chowder

ANDREW G. IANNACCHIONE, CEC, AAC, OWNER, HOSPITALITY REFERRALS/CONSULTANTS, CORPORATE CONSULTING CHEF, U.S. FOODSERVICE, BEDFORD, PA

This recipe was developed for a Clarion Hotel and Conference Center (where recent Middle East peace talks were held) in Sheperdstown, West Virginia, located near the Antietam National Battlefield. It showcases the local produce and crabmeat from nearby Maryland.

MAKES 8 SERVINGS

1/2 cup salt pork

2 celery stalks, diced

2 new potatoes, diced

1 carrot, peeled and diced

1 medium onion, diced

1 green bell pepper, cored, seeded, and diced

2 cloves garlic, minced

2 cups corn kernels (fresh or frozen)

1 cup diced tomatoes

1 1/2 teaspoons Old Bay Seasoning

1 1/2 teaspoons Tabasco sauce

1 1/2 tablespoons Worcestershire sauce

2 bay leaves

Salt and freshly ground black pepper

1/2 cup sweet sherry

1 tablespoon cornstarch

8 cups chicken stock

2 cups heavy cream

8 ounces Maryland crabmeat

1 tablespoon fresh thyme, or 1 teaspoon dried

In a large saucepan, heat the salt pork over medium heat. Cook, stirring often, until pork is lightly browned and fat has been rendered. Remove the salt pork, leaving the fat in the pan.

Add the celery, potatoes, carrot, onion, green pepper, and garlic, and cook until the vegetables are slightly softened and lightly browned, 5 to 7 minutes. Stir in the corn, tomatoes, Old Bay Seasoning, Tabasco sauce, Worcestershire sauce, and bay leaves; season with salt and pepper. Cook, stirring often, 5 minutes, then add 1/4 cup of the sherry. Cook another 2 to 3 minutes, or until the sherry is reduced by about half.

Make a slurry: in a small bowl, whisk together the remaining 1/4 cup sherry and the cornstarch. Stir this slurry into the saucepan, along with the stock. Bring to a boil, then reduce the heat and simmer until thickened, about 5 minutes. Stir in the cream, crabmeat, and thyme; season with salt and pepper.

Cioppino Pasta Fagioli

S. B. "DOC" JENSEN, CEC, CCE, AAC, FORMER PROFESSOR EMERITUS,
ADIRONDACK COMMUNITY COLLEGE, QUEENSBURY, NY

As a restaurant chef with a kitchen staff to feed between seatings, I am always looking for quick and nutritious meals to serve. *Cioppino* is a classic Italian seafood soup recipe, similar to French *bouillabaisse,* that Italian immigrants created in San Francisco. I added beans to make this a delicious and totally satisfying one-pot meal.

MAKES 4 SERVINGS

Twelve ¹/₂-inch-thick slices French bread

2 cloves garlic, lightly crushed

3 tablespoons olive oil

1¹/₂ cups diced onions

1¹/₂ cups diced green bell peppers

2 cloves garlic, minced

1 quart clam juice

3 cups diced canned tomatoes, including juices

8 ounces haddock or cod fillets,
    cut in 2-inch pieces

2 fresh or frozen lobster tails (about 4 ounces
    each), cut in 2 pieces each

8 large shrimp, peeled and deveined

¹/₃ cup small shell pasta

1 tablespoon chopped fresh basil

1 tablespoon chopped flat-leaf parsley

8 ounces sea scallops, abductor muscle
    removed if necessary

One 16-ounce can Great Northern beans,
    rinsed and drained

¹/₃ cup dry white wine

3 dashes Tabasco sauce

Salt and freshly ground black pepper

Preheat the oven to 350°F.

Rub the bread slices with the crushed garlic and place on a baking sheet. Bake for 15 minutes, or until the slices are crispy and just starting to brown. Remove from the oven; set aside.

Heat the olive oil in a large saucepan over medium heat. Add the onions, peppers, and garlic, and cook, stirring, until soft, about 5 minutes. Add the clam juice and the tomatoes with their juices. Stir and bring to a boil. Add the fish and lobster pieces, gently stir to combine, and lower the heat to maintain a low boil. Stir in the shrimp, pasta, basil, and parsley, stir, and cook for 5 minutes. Add the scallops and the beans. Reduce the heat to low, cover the pan, and cook 5 minutes. Add the wine and Tabasco, and season with salt and pepper. Simmer another minute, then serve in shallow soup bowls garnished with 3 slices of toasted bread.

Stewed Lamb Naples Style
(Agnello Spizzato Campania)

GINO A. CORELLI, CEC, AAC, EXECUTIVE CHEF,
BROWN UNIVERSITY FOOD SERVICE, PROVIDENCE, RI

With a considerable Italian immigrant population, Rhode Island is peppered with Italian flavors and traditions. Naples and the surrounding region of Campania are particularly well represented in the state. This recipe combines local lamb, raised extensively in Rhode Island, with the flavors of my heritage.

MAKES 8 SERVINGS

3 pounds lamb shoulder or shanks,
    cut in 2- to 3-inch chunks (if using shanks,
    leave whole, bone in)

Salt and freshly ground black pepper

4 tablespoons olive oil

1 cup red wine, such as Burgundy

1 cup chopped onions

2 medium carrots, peeled and cut into
    $1/2$-inch-thick sticks

$1/2$ cup chopped celery

2 tablespoons minced garlic

$3/4$ cup diced canned Italian-style tomatoes

$1^{1}/_{2}$ teaspoons crushed red pepper flakes

$1/4$ cup chopped flat-leaf parsley

$1/4$ cup chopped fresh chives

Trim most of the visible fat from the lamb and discard. Season the lamb with salt and pepper. In a large sauté pan, heat 3 tablespoons of the olive oil over medium-high heat until almost smoking, about 2 minutes. Add a few pieces of the lamb at a time, turning to brown all over. Remove the pieces as they brown. Add $1/2$ cup of the wine to the pan, stirring to loosen the flavorful bits stuck to the bottom of the pan. Transfer to a deep plate or bowl with the lamb. Set aside.

Clean and thoroughly dry the pan, add the remaining tablespoon of oil, and place over medium heat. After 1 or 2 minutes, add the onions, carrots, celery, and garlic, and cook, stirring, until the onions are softened, about 5 minutes. Add the remaining $1/2$ cup wine, the browned lamb pieces and their juices, and the tomatoes. Season with the red pepper flakes and salt and pepper. Bring to a boil, reduce the heat to low, cover, and simmer, stirring occasionally and adding a little water if necessary, until the lamb pieces are very tender, $1^{1}/_{4}$ to $1^{1}/_{2}$ hours. Stir in the parsley and chives and serve in shallow soup bowls.

Navarin of Lamb

KLAUS MULLER, CCE, AAC, DEAN, ACADEMY OF CULINARY ARTS,
ATLANTIC CAPE COMMUNITY COLLEGE, MAYS LANDING, NJ

After World War II, classically trained European chefs turned to America in search of new opportunities. They brought with them countless classic dishes from their homelands. *Navarin* is a traditional French ragout, familiar to Americans as lamb stew. This hearty dish can be prepared with the meat and vegetables in one pot; however, the vegetables will all turn brown. By boiling the vegetables separately, you can use their leftover cooking liquid in the stew, and the vegetables will maintain their original colors.

MAKES 4 TO 6 SERVINGS

3 carrots, peeled

2 small turnips, peeled

1 medium potato, peeled

Salt

2 tablespoons vegetable oil

1$^1/_2$ pounds lamb shoulder, cut into 1$^1/_2$-inch cubes

Freshly ground black pepper

2 celery stalks, cut into 1-inch segments

1 large onion, sliced

1 clove garlic, minced

2 tablespoons tomato paste

$^1/_2$ tablespoon paprika

$^1/_2$ teaspoon dried rosemary

$^1/_8$ teaspoon dried thyme

$^1/_4$ cup all-purpose flour

1 quart brown stock or water

1 tablespoon chopped flat-leaf parsley

Bring a large pot of water to a boil. Cut the carrots, turnips and potatoes into $^1/_2$-inch dice. Salt the boiling water and add the vegetables. Cook until tender, about 20 minutes. Drain the vegetables, reserving 1 quart of the cooking water to add to the stew later. Keep the vegetables warm.

Heat the oil in a Dutch oven or a large deep sauté pan over medium-high heat. Season the lamb with salt and pepper, and cook, turning the pieces as they brown, until all sides are evenly browned, 8 to 10 minutes. Add the celery, onion, and garlic and cook, stirring, 2 to 3 minutes. Add the tomato paste, paprika, rosemary, and thyme, and cook, stirring constantly, until it begins to brown, 1 to 2 minutes. Sprinkle the flour over top, stir, and cook another minute. Add the reserved vegetable cooking liquid, and bring to a boil. Reduce the heat to low, cover, and cook, stirring often, until the lamb is very tender, about 1 hour.

Skim any fat from the surface of the stew. Adjust the seasoning with salt and pepper. Serve the lamb stew into bowls, and top each serving with vegetables. Sprinkle with the parsley and serve.

Venison Ragout

WILLI DAFFINGER, CEC, AAC, EXECUTIVE CHEF,
ROLLING ROCK CLUB, LIGONIER, PA

I first learned this recipe while working as an apprentice in Munich. I was later happy to find that it's so well suited to the local ingredients in Western Pennsylvania. The region is terrific for fishing and game hunting. This ragout will be just as delicious made with farm-raised venison, but it's perfect for the wild variety—the cooking time can be increased if the meat seems tough. Another way to ensure your venison will be tender is to soak the meat in buttermilk overnight before cooking.

MAKES 8 SERVINGS

¼ cup bacon fat or vegetable oil

2 large onions, diced

3 pounds venison shoulder, cut into 1½-inch cubes

1 teaspoon paprika

¼ teaspoon ground caraway seeds

¼ teaspoon ground juniper berries

Salt and freshly ground black pepper

3 tablespoons all-purpose flour

1 to 1½ pounds mushrooms (any type is fine), quartered

1½ cups dry red wine, such as merlot or cabernet

1½ cups beef or chicken stock, hot

2 bay leaves

Grated zest of ½ lemon

Heat the fat or oil in a large sauté pan over medium heat. When melted, add the onions and cook, stirring, until softened, about 5 minutes. Sprinkle the venison with the paprika, caraway seeds, juniper berries, and salt and pepper. Dredge the meat pieces in the flour, shaking off the excess. As they're finished, place them into the pan, and cook until browned on all sides. Add the mushrooms to the pan and cook, stirring, 2 to 3 minutes. Add the wine and cook for a few minutes to reduce by two-thirds. Add the stock and the bay leaves and bring to a boil. Reduce the heat to low, cover, and simmer 30 minutes, or until the venison is tender. Stir in the lemon zest. Adjust the seasoning with salt and pepper.

Country-Style Chicken Stew

FRITZ SONNENSCHMIDT, CMC, AAC, CULINARY DEAN,
THE CULINARY INSTITUTE OF AMERICA, HYDE PARK, NY

The Delaware-Maryland area, known as Delmarva, is famous for its chicken farms. Frank Perdue and other chicken companies are based there. Use regional red wine, and farm-fresh ingredients, and this dish will taste straight from the chicken farmer's table.

MAKES 6 SERVINGS

10 black peppercorns

6 juniper berries, crushed, optional

1 bay leaf

1 fresh thyme sprig

6 whole chicken legs, thigh attached

Salt and freshly ground black pepper

6 celery stalks, thinly sliced

2 carrots, peeled and thinly sliced

2 medium red onions, chopped

4 cups chicken stock

1 bottle (750 ml) plus 1 cup dry red wine,
    such as Burgundy or Bordeaux

8 ounces slab bacon, cut into small cubes

3 to 4 tablespoons ketchup

2 potatoes, peeled and cubed

6 cloves garlic, crushed

8 ounces white button mushrooms, quartered

$^{1}/_{4}$ cup all-purpose flour

$^{1}/_{2}$ cup sliced scallions

To prepare a *bouquet garni* (herb bouquet), place the peppercorns, juniper berries, bay leaf, and thyme sprig in the center of a piece of cheesecloth. Tie securely closed and set aside.

Cut each chicken leg into two pieces at the joint between the thigh and the drumstick. Season the chicken pieces with salt and pepper and place them in a roasting pan. Add the celery, carrots, onions, chicken stock, and bottle of red wine. Add the bouquet garni. Cover with plastic wrap, and refrigerate at least 8 hours or overnight.

Preheat the grill. Remove the chicken from the marinade and pat dry. When the grill is very hot, rub the rack lightly with oil and place the chicken pieces on top, skin side down. Cook the chicken, 2 to 3 minutes, or until nicely grill marked, but not cooked through. Transfer to a platter.

Remove the bouquet garni from the marinade in the roasting pan. Place the marinade onto the grill rack and close the grill. When the marinade comes to a boil, stir in the bacon, ketchup, potatoes, garlic, and mushrooms. Add the chicken pieces and adjust the grill heat so that the liquid just simmers. Cover the grill and cook for 1 hour.

Combine the remaining 1 cup of red wine with the flour, mixing until well blended. Using a large fork or kitchen tongs, remove the chicken from the sauce, and stir in the red wine-flour mixture. Cook, stirring, for 10 minutes, until slightly thickened. Remove the pan from the heat, and return the chicken pieces to the pan. Spoon the sauce over top to warm. Set aside for 10 minutes, then serve sprinkled with scallion slices.

Cajun Sausage Stew

LOUIS JESOWSKEK, CEC, AAC, DIRECTOR OF FOOD AND NUTRITION SERVICES,
OUR LADY OF THE LAKE REGIONAL MEDICAL CENTER, BATON ROUGE, LA

Cajun customs and cooking continue to thrive in Livingston Parish, a many-centuries-old French-speaking community in southern Louisiana. The tradition of *la boucherie* (hog butchering) exemplifies the prudent tradition of utilizing all parts of the animal. Delicacies include *sulze* (hog-head cheese), *gratons* (cracklings), *guag* (stuffed stomach), *boudin noir* (blood sausage), and the smoked sausage highlighted in this stew. Cajun smoked sausage is a rich mahogany color and offers double-smoked flavor. Serve with slices of French bread and a cold Dixie beer.

MAKES 6 SERVINGS

2 pounds spicy, smoked sausage (Cajun-flavored would be best), cut in ¹/₂-inch rounds

2 celery stalks, diced

1 onion, diced

1 green bell pepper, stemmed, seeded and diced

2 tablespoons tomato paste

¹/₄ cup all-purpose flour

2 cups chicken stock

1 teaspoon fresh chopped thyme, or ¹/₂ teaspoon dried

6 red bliss potatoes, halved

2 small sweet potatoes, peeled and cut in 1¹/₂-inch cubes

2 carrots, peeled and diced

2 turnips, peeled and cut in 1-inch cubes

Salt, freshly ground black pepper, and cayenne pepper

1 cup pearl onions, peeled (see note)

Preheat the oven to 350°F.

In a large cast-iron Dutch oven, cook the sausage over medium heat, stirring often, until sausage is browned and fat is rendered, about 8 minutes. Using tongs or a slotted spoon, remove the sausage pieces and set aside.

Add the celery, onion, and pepper to the pan and cook, stirring often, until the onion browns, about 5 minutes. Add the tomato paste and cook, stirring constantly, until it turns a rusty color, about 30 seconds. Add the flour and cook, stirring constantly, 3 minutes.

Pour in ²/₃ cup of the chicken stock and whisk to dissolve any lumps. Add the remaining chicken stock along with the thyme and the reserved sausage. Bring to boil, cover, and cook until the sausage is very tender, about 20 minutes.

Add the potatoes, sweet potatoes, carrots, and turnips. Season with salt, black pepper, and cayenne. Cook, 20 minutes, then add the pearl onions. Cook, 10 minutes, or until all of the vegetables are tender.

TO PEEL PEARL ONIONS:

Make a small X in the root end of each onion. Drop them into a small pot of boiling water and cook for 3 minutes. Drain, rinse under cold water, and drain again. They can now be easily peeled.

Jalapeño Smokehouse Stew

S. B. "DOC" JENSEN, CEC, CCE, AAC, FORMER PROFESSOR EMERITUS, ADIRONDACK COMMUNITY COLLEGE, QUEENSBURY, NY

Though French in origin, andouille sausage has become an American specialty. It is the base of classic Cajun dishes such as gumbo and jambalaya, and has grown tremendously in popularity since the 1980s when the cooking of New Orleans rose to national fame. Use any smoked sausage in this recipe, such as smokehouse kielbasa.

MAKES 4 SERVINGS

1 tablespoon olive oil

4 chicken legs

½ pound boneless, skinless chicken breasts, cut in 2-inch-long pieces

8 ounces smoked sausage, sliced ¾-inch thick

4 celery stalks, cut in 1-inch pieces

3 medium jalapeño peppers, seeded and minced

2 large carrots, peeled, halved lengthwise and sliced in 1-inch-thick half-moons

2 large shallots, minced

1 tablespoon minced garlic

1 teaspoon saffron

2 teaspoons salt, or to taste

1 teaspoon freshly ground black pepper

½ teaspoon barbecue spice (available in the supermarket spice section)

5 cups chicken broth

1½ cups long-grain white rice

1 large yellow bell pepper, cut into 1-inch pieces

4 ounces sugar-snap peas, cut into thirds on the bias

1 tablespoon chopped flat-leaf parsley

Heat the olive oil in a large saucepan over medium-high heat. Add the chicken legs and meat and brown on both sides. Transfer to a platter and set aside.

Add the sausage to the pan and cook, stirring often, until the sausage is browned, about 5 minutes. Add the celery, jalapeño peppers, carrots, shallots, garlic, and saffron. Season with the salt, pepper, and barbecue spice. Add the broth, bring to a boil, then reduce the heat to simmer. Return the chicken to the pan, cover, and simmer for 20 minutes.

Add the rice and bell peppers, and simmer 30 minutes, adding the peas during the last 5 minutes. To serve, divide the rice and vegetables among the serving bowls, place a chicken leg and a slice of breast meat into each, and spoon the broth over top. Garnish each serving with a pinch of chopped parsley.

CHAPTER TWO

Sides &
Salads

An Abundance of Fresh Ingredients

from America's Farms and Gardens

A MEAL CAN LEAP FROM THE ORDINARY TO THE spectacular on the strength of its accompaniments—salads, appetizers, and side dishes. Be it soup and salad, chicken and dumplings, or a hamburger with fries, most main courses demand accompaniments to make the meal complete.

The refreshing and intriguing salads in this chapter utilize ingredients from around the corner and around the world: Kona Lobster and Papaya Salad with Tropical Fruit Dressing features native Hawaiian ingredients; the Vermont Country Salad is made with local maple syrup and cheddar cheese; and the Warm Farmers' Market Potato Salad is inspired by the green markets

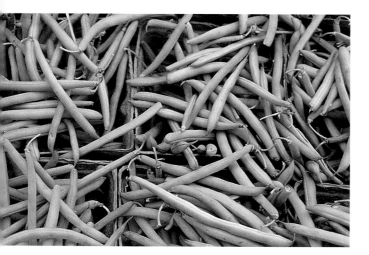

across the country that make fresh, local ingredients available to the home cook.

Appetizers and side dishes are the supporting players for the meal to come; they also give the home cook a chance to experiment with unfamiliar ingredients and cooking techniques that might be too daunting to master for a main course: the Golden Wrap is prepared with spring-roll wrappers and Chinese oyster sauce; Basil-Pesto-Spinach Timbales are an exotic accompaniment for roasted meats or fowl; the Carpaccio of Radish uses a classic Italian technique to prepare daikon, an Asian radish; and the Turtle Bay Estate Potato Pancakes pair traditionally-inspired potato pancakes, made here with a combination of white and sweet potatoes, with a sauce of tropical guava, apples and cinnamon. All of the dishes in this chapter provide an opportunity to encounter a variety of new tastes inspired by America's culinary melting pot.

Warm Spinach, Fig, and Tasso Salad with Honey Balsamic Vinaigrette

VINCENT ALBERICI, AAC, EXECUTIVE CHEF,
ADAM'S MARK HOTEL, PHILADELPHIA, PA

This dish was created to combine two of the foods I enjoy most, leafy greens and figs. Ordinarily, my heritage would lead me to pair the sweet figs and earthy spinach with Italian prosciutto or pancetta. *Tasso* is a Cajun smoked-meat specialty, made from pork or beef, with just enough red pepper and garlic added to make this salad unique. You may have a hard time finding tasso outside Louisiana, but you can substitute prosciutto instead.

MAKES 6 SERVINGS

12 ounces fresh spinach

1/4 cup olive oil

3 tablespoons minced shallots

1 1/2 tablespoons minced garlic

1/2 cup julienned red onion

2 ounces tasso, diced small

2 tablespoons honey

1 cup chicken stock

1/4 cup balsamic vinegar

1/4 cup extra-virgin olive oil

6 sliced fresh figs

Kosher salt and freshly ground white pepper

Clean and rinse the spinach leaves and keep them in the refrigerator until ready to use. Chill the serving plates too, if possible.

In a medium sauté pan over medium-high heat, add the olive oil, shallots, and garlic and cook, stirring, 45 seconds. Add the red onion and cook, stirring, 1 minute more. Add the tasso and toss just until hot. Add the honey, bring to a boil, reduce the heat and simmer, 2 minutes.

Add the chicken stock and vinegar to the pan to deglaze, scraping up any flavorful bits stuck to the bottom of the pan. Bring to a boil, reduce the heat and simmer until the liquids are reduced by one-quarter, about 5 minutes.

Remove the pan from the heat, drizzle in the extra-virgin olive oil, add the sliced figs and salt and pepper to taste, and stir.

Distribute the spinach leaves among the serving plates. Spoon some of the warm ham and fig vinaigrette over each serving.

Vermont Country Salad

GERALD P. BONSEY, CEC, AAC, EXECUTIVE CHEF,
THE YORK HARBOR INN, YORK HARBOR, ME

Native-Americans are credited with discovering maple sugar, or Indian Sugar. Early colonists depended on it as their primary sweetener, and used it as a trading commodity. Sugaring was an integral part of early dairy farms, providing work during the winter and spring and hard cash for seed and fertilizer. The demand for maple sugar diminished when improved transportation increased the availability of cane sugar. Production gradually shifted to maple syrup, an industry that thrives in Vermont today.

MAKES 4 SERVINGS

3 tablespoons maple syrup

¼ cup apple-cider vinegar

1 teaspoon Dijon mustard

1 teaspoon minced garlic

½ cup vegetable oil

½ teaspoon salt

¼ teaspoon freshly ground black pepper

6 slices uncooked bacon

½ pound mixed baby greens

1 cup shredded cheddar cheese

1 cup croutons

To prepare the vinaigrette, combine the syrup, vinegar, mustard, and garlic in a small bowl. Add the oil in a steady stream, whisking constantly. Season with the salt and pepper and set aside.

Place the bacon in one layer in a skillet and set over medium heat. Cook, turning once or twice, until crispy, 5 to 7 minutes. Transfer to a paper towel-lined plate and let cool slightly. Crumble.

In a large mixing bowl, combine the greens, cheddar cheese, croutons, and the bacon. Pour the vinaigrette over the top and toss to combine. Place a neat mound on each plate and serve immediately.

Salad of Frisée and Tangerine with Grilled Sweet Potato

FRITZ SONNENSCHMIDT, CMC, AAC, CULINARY DEAN,
THE CULINARY INSTITUTE OF AMERICA, HYDE PARK, NY

If you already enjoy sweet potatoes, you'll love them grilled. The sweet potato originated in South America, but has been a staple of Southern-style cooking in the United States since the seventeenth century. It's often mistakenly called a yam, particularly in reference to favorite holiday dishes like candied yams. Actually, the yam comes from an entirely different plant species, grown primarily in Africa. It's very unlikely that you'll find it for sale in this country except in ethnic specialty markets.

MAKES 6 SERVINGS

2 medium sweet potatoes, well rinsed

$^3/_4$ cup olive or peanut oil

$^1/_4$ cup flat-leaf parsley leaves

3 tablespoons soy sauce

2 tablespoons orange juice

5 cloves garlic, crushed

4 tangerines, peeled, sectioned, membranes removed

$^1/_4$ cup white wine, such as Riesling or chardonnay

2 tablespoons honey mustard

1 tablespoon balsamic vinegar

1 teaspoon poppy seeds, toasted

1 tablespoon chopped fresh chervil, or $^1/_2$ teaspoon dried

Salt and freshly ground black pepper

1 head frisée, cored, well rinsed, and spun dry

Preheat the oven to 350°F.

Bake or boil the sweet potatoes until they are $^3/_4$ cooked, about 20 minutes; a sharp knife should enter the flesh with a little resistance. Let cool slightly, peel and discard the skin, and slice into $^1/_4$-inch-thick rounds.

In a medium bowl, combine $^1/_4$ cup of the oil, the parsley, soy sauce, orange juice, and crushed garlic. Stir to combine, add the sweet potato slices, moving and turning them to coat evenly. Set aside for at least 10 minutes or up to 1 hour.

Preheat the grill. When hot, brush the grill rack with oil. Add the sweet potato slices and cook on both sides until just cooked through.

To prepare the dressing, combine the remaining $^1/_2$ cup oil, white wine, honey mustard, balsamic vinegar, and poppy seeds in a large bowl. Whisk to blend. Add the tangerine segments and chervil; season with salt and pepper. Fold in the frisée, evenly coating with the dressing. Portion the salad onto 6 serving plates. Top with the grilled sweet potato slices.

TO TOAST THE POPPY SEEDS:

Place the poppy seeds in a skillet over medium-low heat and cook, stirring frequently to prevent burning, until fragrant and lightly toasted, about 2 minutes.

Warm Farmers' Market Potato Salad

RUDY GARCIA, CEC, AAC, EXECUTIVE CHEF, CULINARY ARTS, LOS ANGELES MISSION COLLEGE, LOS ANGELES, CA

I conduct cooking demonstrations at the farmers' market in Encino, and that's where I created this recipe, a new interpretation of a classic. I cooked the potatoes, and added whatever ingredients looked best at the market that day. The result is a light, fresh, and contemporary salad, which can be served as is, or as an entrée topped with grilled breast of chicken. In place of the new and Yukon Gold potatoes, you may substitute Peruvian purple, Russets, or Russian finger potatoes.

MAKES 8 SERVINGS

1 1/2 pounds new potatoes

1 1/2 pounds Yukon Gold potatoes

1 cup Pecan Crunch (see note), coarsely chopped

1/2 cup honey

1/4 cup balsamic vinegar

1/4 cup apple cider

1/2 teaspoon celery seeds

1/2 teaspoon onion powder

2 tomatoes, diced

2 tablespoons chopped fresh basil

Salt and freshly ground black pepper

Bring a large pot of water to a boil and salt it. Peel the potatoes, then cut them into bite-sized pieces. Transfer the potatoes to the water, and cook until tender but still firm, about 15 minutes. Drain. Transfer to a large bowl and set aside.

In a small bowl, whisk together the honey, balsamic vinegar, apple cider, celery seeds, and onion powder. Add this mixture to the bowl with the potatoes, along with the tomatoes and basil. Season with salt and pepper. Gently stir to combine. Serve warm or at room temperature.

TO MAKE THE PECAN CRUNCH:

Heat 1/2 cup sugar in a heavy saucepan over medium heat, stirring constantly, until it melts and just starts to brown. Add 1 cup of whole pecans to the caramelized sugar, stir to coat well. Cook, stirring, until the pecans are colored, but before the sugar burns, 2 to 3 minutes. Let cool.

The Golden Wrap

MARTIN YAN, AAC, YAN CAN COOK, INC.

I grew up eating these treasures during New Years' celebrations, where their resemblance to gold bars made them popular with anyone hoping for a prosperous year ahead. However, there's no need to wait months for their magic to take effect, because these treats give your tummy an instant gratification right on the spot. You can serve them with store-bought sweet-and-sour or hot mustard sauces, if you'd like.

MAKES 8 TO 10 ROLLS

$2\frac{1}{2}$ tablespoons peanut oil, plus 2 to 3 cups for deep frying

2 large eggs, lightly beaten

$\frac{1}{2}$ pound boneless beef or chicken, cut into thin strips

6 shiitake mushrooms, stems discarded, caps thinly sliced

2 cups shredded green cabbage

2 scallions, cut into 1-inch segments

$\frac{1}{4}$ cup thinly sliced bamboo shoots, fresh or canned

2 tablespoons Chinese oyster sauce

$1\frac{1}{2}$ teaspoons cornstarch

8 to 10 spring roll wrappers

Place a large, nonstick skillet or wok over medium-high heat. Add $\frac{1}{2}$ tablespoon peanut oil, swirling to evenly coat the bottom and sides. Pour the beaten eggs into the pan, and tilt pan to evenly coat the bottom. Cook $1\frac{1}{2}$ minutes, or until the top is set and the bottom is lightly browned. Slide the eggs out of pan onto a cutting board, and slice into 1-inch long strips. Set aside.

Wipe the skillet clean and place it over high heat. When the pan is hot, add 2 tablespoons oil, swirling to coat the pan. Add the meat and cook, stirring, 2 minutes. Add the mushrooms, cabbage, scallions, bamboo shoots, and oyster sauce. Cook, stirring, another 2 minutes; dust with the cornstarch. Cook 1 to 2 minutes, until the sauce thickens.

Remove the pan from the heat, stir in the egg strips, and set aside to cool.

To fill, place 1 egg-roll wrapper on a work surface. Spoon 2 heaping tablespoons of the filling in 3-inch-long log down the center of the wrapper. Fold the bottom of the wrapper over the filling, then fold in the sides of the wrapper over the filling. Brush the top edge of the wrapper with water. Roll up tightly, pressing to seal the edge. Repeat with the remaining wrappers and filling mixture. Cover the rolls with a towel until ready to fry. (The rolls can be made 6 hours ahead; keep them covered and chilled.)

Heat the remaining 2 to 3 cups oil over medium-high heat in a Dutch oven or deep sauté pan. When the oil reaches 360°F, deep-fry the spring rolls, 2 to 3 at a time, turning occasionally, until golden, 2 to 3 minutes. Using a slotted spoon, transfer the cooked spring rolls to a paper towel-lined plate.

Basil Pesto Spinach Timbale

JOHN R. FISHER, CEC, AAC, ACADEMIC DEPARTMENT DIRECTOR CULINARY ARTS, THE ART INSTITUTE OF SEATTLE, SEATTLE, WA

A *timbale* (pronounced TIM-bul) is a soft or creamy dish that is cooked in a mold, and turned out onto the plate for serving, making for a dramatic presentation. This recipe was created to accompany the Sesame Chicken over Northern White Bean Ragout on page 72. The timbale's soft and savory texture offers a wonderful contrast to that hearty dish. You can serve this side dish with sautéed or grilled beef as well. My inspiration is simple—spinach and basil are just wonderful in the late spring and early summer.

MAKES 6 SERVINGS

16 to 20 spinach leaves

1 teaspoon butter

2 large eggs

$^1/_2$ cup heavy cream

$^1/_4$ cup prepared basil pesto (available in most gourmet stores and supermarkets, or prepare your own)

Pinch ground cinnamon and ground nutmeg

Salt and freshly ground white pepper

Preheat the oven to 350°F.

Bring a large pot of salted water to a boil. Add the spinach leaves and blanch, 30 seconds to 1 minute, until wilted. Drain. When the leaves are cool enough to handle, gently squeeze out the excess water.

Rub six 4-ounce ramekins with butter, then line them with the spinach leaves, reserving 6 leaves. In a medium bowl, beat the eggs. Stir in the cream, pesto, and spices; season with salt and pepper. Pour the custard into the spinach-lined cups, and cover each with one of the remaining spinach leaves. Place the ramekins into a baking pan, and add enough hot water to come halfway up the sides. Place in the oven until the custard is set, 25 to 30 minutes. Let rest for 5 minutes before serving.

Creamed Chanterelles

FRITZ SONNENSCHMIDT, CMC, AAC, CULINARY DEAN,
THE CULINARY INSTITUTE OF AMERICA, HYDE PARK, NY

Although they are predominantly imported from France, fresh chanterelle mushrooms are cultivated in the Pacific Northwest and along the East Coast, particularly in Pennsylvania and the Hudson Valley area. They are typically available from early summer through mid-winter, and lend a meaty, flowery, nutty taste to the dishes that they grace. The bright yellow to orange color and trumpet shape of chanterelles make for attractive additions to any plate, although you may substitute white button mushrooms if chanterelles are unavailable. I recommend serving this creamy mushroom ragout with veal, beef, chicken, or turkey, and even over pasta.

MAKES 6 SERVINGS

¼ cup (½ stick) butter

3 shallots, finely diced

1½ pounds chanterelle mushrooms,
   brushed clean

Salt and freshly ground black pepper

½ cup heavy cream or sour cream

1 teaspoon chopped fresh chives

Heat the butter in a large sauté pan with a lid over medium-high heat. When bubbly, add the shallots and chanterelles, season with salt and pepper, and cook, stirring, until the shallots are transparent, 1 to 2 minutes. Reduce the heat to low, cover, and braise the mushrooms for 5 minutes. Remove the lid and cook until any released liquid has evaporated. Stir in the heavy or sour cream. When the mixture simmers, remove it from the heat. Stir in the chives.

Soba Noodle Salad

STAFFORD T. DE CAMBRA, CEC, CCE, AAC, SENIOR EXECUTIVE CHEF,
S.S. INDEPENDENCE, AMERICAN HAWAII CRUISES

Buckwheat soba noodles are very common in Japanese cuisine, and are paired here with traditional Chinese ingredients like oyster sauce, scallions, and sesame oil for a new combination of flavors, representative of Hawaii's varied Asian population. Though this salad is good enough to eat on its own, you might also pair it in a decorative way with favorite ingredients like Chinese *char sui* pork, Japanese *kamabuko* or teriyaki yellowfin tuna, or Hawaiian smoked *ono* and *maki* sushi.

MAKES 4 SERVINGS

FOR THE DRESSING:

1 cup chicken stock

$1/2$ cup Chinese oyster sauce

$1/2$ cup thinly sliced scallions

2 tablespoons reduced-sodium soy sauce

2 tablespoons sesame oil

1 teaspoon freshly squeezed lemon juice

1 teaspoon fresh orange juice

Salt and freshly ground black pepper

FOR THE SALAD:

1 tablespoon peanut oil

2 large eggs

2 tablespoons milk

Salt and freshly ground black pepper

12 ounces dry soba (buckwheat) noodles

1 cup julienned ham

1 cup julienned shiitake mushroom caps

$1/4$ cup thinly sliced red onion

$1/4$ cup julienned red bell pepper

$1/4$ cup julienned carrots

$1/4$ cup julienned snow peas

$1/4$ cup julienned *kamabuko* (see note)

$1/4$ cup sliced scallions

To prepare the dressing, combine all of the ingredients in a small bowl, mix well, and set aside.

Bring a large pot of water to a boil and generously salt it.

Prepare a quick omelet: Heat the peanut oil in an 8-inch skillet, preferably nonstick, over medium-high heat. In a small bowl, beat the eggs and milk; season with salt and pepper. Swirl the oil around the pan to coat, and pour in the egg mixture. Cook undisturbed for 30 seconds, then, using a spatula, push the sides of the omelet towards the center, tilting the pan to let the runny center flow out to the perimeter. Lower the heat to medium and repeat until the eggs are set, about 2 minutes. Transfer the omelet to a clean cutting board and let cool slightly. Slice the omelet in half, then cut each half into long thin strips. Set aside.

Place the soba noodles in the boiling water and cook until tender, 3 to 4 minutes. Drain and immediately rinse the noodles under cold water. Drain again, then transfer to a large bowl.

Add the ham, mushrooms, red onion, red pepper, carrot, and snow peas to the noodles, with $3/4$ cup of the dressing, and toss or gently stir to combine. Adjust the seasoning with salt and pepper, if necessary.

Place the soba salad onto a large platter or in a serving bowl and garnish with *kamabuko*, scallions, and egg slices.

ABOUT KAMABUKO

Kamabuko is a type of prepared fish cake available in many Asian markets. It looks and feels a little like *surimi*, imitation crabmeat, which would be a good substitute if kamabuko is unavailable.

Kona Lobster and Papaya Salad with Tropical Fruit Dressing

STAFFORD T. DE CAMBRA, CEC, CCE, AAC, SENIOR EXECUTIVE CHEF,
S.S. INDEPENDENCE, AMERICAN HAWAII CRUISES

This recipe brings the mountains and the sea together—sweet, spiny lobster from Kona, my home, combined with papaya, which is locally grown on Hawaii. If you can't find papaya in your part of the country, mango would make a delicious substitute. The lobster and papaya, each delicate in flavor on their own, become infused with the vibrant flavor of the citrus-based dressing.

MAKES 4 SERVINGS

FOR THE DRESSING:

3/4 cup sugar

1/4 cup cornstarch

4 large eggs

1 cup orange juice

1 cup pineapple juice

1/2 cup fresh lime juice (6 to 7 limes)

1 cup sour cream

FOR THE SALAD:

8 ounces Kona Coast lobster meat, cut into chunks and chilled (Maine lobster meat may be substituted)

2 papayas, peeled, seeded, and diced

1 Maui onion, finely minced (1 Vidalia onion may be substituted)

2 tablespoons diced tomato

1 tablespoon chopped fresh mint leaves

8 Belgium endive leaves

1 teaspoon black sesame seeds, optional

TO MAKE THE DRESSING:

In a medium bowl, mix together the sugar and the cornstarch until well blended. Add the eggs and beat until smooth.

Combine the orange, pineapple and lime juice in a medium saucepan and bring to a boil. Remove from the heat and slowly add the juice to the egg mixture, whisking constantly. Return to the saucepan and bring to a boil, stirring constantly. Reduce the heat to low and simmer, stirring, until thickened, 2 to 3 minutes. Transfer to a clean bowl and chill.

When the dressing is cold, beat in the sour cream. Cover and refrigerate.

TO MAKE THE SALAD:

In a large bowl, combine the lobster, papaya, onions, tomatoes, and mint. Toss or gently stir to incorporate. Add 3/4 of the salad dressing and stir to blend.

For a dramatic presentation, line 4 martini glasses with 2 endive leaves each. Portion the lobster mixture into the glasses. Sprinkle with the black sesame seeds, if using, and serve.

Grilled Celeriac and Portobello Mushrooms

FRITZ SONNENSCHMIDT, CMC, AAC, CULINARY DEAN,
THE CULINARY INSTITUTE OF AMERICA, HYDE PARK, NY

Celeriac, also known as celery root, is a root vegetable, and its culinary use in America dates back to early revolutionary days. Colonists kept root cellars to store carrots, turnips, rutabagas, and other vegetables over the winter. Celeriac is a tasty and versatile vegetable, and can be boiled and braised, or made into soups and even salads. Colonists may have cooked celeriac over an open fire, so why not cook it on the grill? Portobellos have grown tremendously popular in the last few years, and can be found in supermarkets everywhere. Removing the gills from the underside of the portobellos is for appearance only, and isn't necessary to improve the taste of this dish.

MAKES 6 SERVINGS

2 small celeriac

Juice of 2 lemons

$\frac{1}{2}$ teaspoon salt

$\frac{1}{2}$ pound portobello mushrooms (select those with small caps), stems reserved for another use

2 tablespoons olive oil

Salt and freshly ground black and white pepper

$\frac{1}{3}$ cup chicken stock

$\frac{1}{4}$ cup butter

$\frac{1}{2}$ teaspoon fresh chopped thyme, or $\frac{1}{4}$ teaspoon dried

Preheat the grill.

Using a sharp paring knife, peel the celeriac. To get to the tasty tender part, you will lose a fair amount of flesh. Place the celeriac into a medium saucepan, add half the lemon juice, and the salt, and cover with water. Bring to a boil and cook until tender, but still firm, about 30 minutes. They are done when a fork can be inserted easily.

Using a paring knife, shave off the underside gills of the portobello mushroom caps, if desired. Brush the caps with olive oil, season with salt and pepper, and place them on the grill, about 4 inches from the heat source. Cook, turning frequently, until they are nicely brown and tender, 4 to 5 minutes per side. Transfer to a plate to cool slightly.

When the celeriac is cool enough to handle, cut into $\frac{1}{2}$-inch-thick slices. Slice the portobello mushroom, on the bias, into $\frac{1}{2}$-inch-thick slices. Arrange the celeriac and portobello slices on serving plates; set aside.

In a small saucepan, bring the chicken stock and remaining lemon juice to a boil. Remove from the heat and whisk in the butter and thyme; season with salt and pepper. Using a hand-held blender or in the bowl of a blender or food processor, whip the sauce until emulsified. Spoon the sauce over the vegetables.

Sausage-Stuffed Artichoke

KLAUS MULLER, CCE, AAC, DEAN, ACADEMY OF CULINARY ARTS,
ATLANTIC CAPE COMMUNITY COLLEGE, MAYS LANDING, NJ

The artichoke is one of many ingredients transplanted by immigrants that have become American favorites. It originates in the Mediterranean region, and has been a staple of Italian, Greek, and Spanish cooking for centuries. Traditionally, artichokes are served with a hollandaise sauce or vinaigrette for dipping, but this recipe offers a heartier way to enjoy this versatile vegetable.

MAKES 3 SERVINGS

3 artichokes

3 slices lemon

Salt

2 tablespoons chicken fat or butter

$1/2$ small onion, diced

8 ounces fresh pork sausage, crumbled

$1/2$ teaspoon fresh chopped thyme

$1/4$ teaspoon fresh chopped sage

1 cup unseasoned dried breadcrumbs

2 tablespoons freshly grated Parmesan cheese

1 large egg, lightly beaten

1 tablespoon chopped fresh flat-leaf parsley

Freshly ground black pepper

1 cup chicken stock

Bring a large pot of water to a boil.

Using a large knife, trim the top $1/2$ inch from the artichokes and discard. Cut off the stem even with the base. Starting at the base, snap off tough outer leaves where they break naturally. Using a paring knife, trim the outside of the base until no dark green areas remain. Tie the lemon slices to the bottom of each artichoke with butcher's twine.

Season the boiling water with salt and add the artichokes. Blanch until they are half cooked, about 10 minutes. Remove from the water and drain them upside down. Remove and discard the lemon and string. Cut off the top half of the artichoke and roughly chop. Gently pull out the center leaves until you see the inner cavity. Using a small spoon, remove the hairy choke and discard.

Heat the chicken fat or butter in a medium skillet over medium heat. Add the onion and cook, stirring, 2 to 3 minutes, but do not brown. Add the sausage meat, chopped artichokes, thyme, and sage, and cook, stirring, until the sausage is cooked. Remove from the heat, stir in the breadcrumbs, grated cheese, egg, and parsley; season with salt and pepper.

Stuff the cavities of the artichokes with the sausage filling. Place them in a saucepan just large enough to hold them in one layer. Pour the chicken stock in the pan and bring to a boil. Reduce the heat to low, cover, and cook until the artichokes are tender, 15 to 20 minutes. Add a little more stock if necessary during cooking.

Carpaccio of Radish

FRITZ SONNENSCHMIDT, CMC, AAC, CULINARY DEAN,
THE CULINARY INSTITUTE OF AMERICA, HYDE PARK, NY

The *daikon* is a member of the radish family, and has recently become quite popular in the United States. You should be able to find it in most Asian markets, and in Chinatowns across the country. *Carpaccio* is a classic Italian preparation of very thinly sliced raw beef, served with a mayonnaise or vinegar sauce. I've adapted the method for this totally vegan recipe, proving that meatless cooking is anything but boring.

MAKES 4 SERVINGS

1 tablespoon sunflower seeds

1 small clove garlic

¼ teaspoon coarse salt

2 tablespoons apple-cider vinegar

½ teaspoon honey

Grated zest of ½ lemon

8 ounces daikon radish, peeled

½-inch-piece peeled ginger, shredded

2 tablespoons hazelnut oil

Place the sunflower seeds in a small skillet and place over medium heat. Cook, tossing or stirring, until lightly browned and fragrant, 2 to 5 minutes. Set aside.

Using the flat side of a large knife, mash the garlic with the salt until it forms a paste. Combine the garlic, vinegar, honey, and the lemon zest in a small saucepan; bring to a boil. Remove from the heat, set aside, and cover to keep warm.

Using a mandoline or slicer set on the finest setting, slice the radish paper thin. Spread the radishes in one layer on the serving plates and pour the warm marinade over them. Sprinkle with the shredded ginger and sunflower seeds. Drizzle with the hazelnut oil.

Asparagus Cheese Straws

KLAUS FRIEDENREICH, CMC, AAC,

THE ART INSTITUTE OF FORT LAUDERDALE, FORT LAUDERDALE, FL

In my homeland, Germany, asparagus is very popular and featured as a special item on restaurant menus when it comes into season. In recent years, asparagus has become equally popular in America. This recipe, an adaptation of a classic technique, was developed for a late-spring or early-summer menu, when asparagus is at its best. Fortunately, you can enjoy this recipe, whenever you'd like, now that asparagus has become available in supermarkets almost all year round.

MAKES 4 SERVINGS

3 asparagus spears

1 cup all-purpose flour

$1/4$ cup ($1/2$ stick) butter, cold, cut into small pieces

$1/3$ cup grated Parmesan cheese

Pinch baking powder

1 large egg plus 1 large egg yolk

Preheat the oven to 450°F.

Place the asparagus, with $1/4$ cup of water, in a medium sauté pan with a lid, set over medium heat. Steam the asparagus until very tender, about 5 minutes. Transfer the asparagus and the cooking liquid to the work bowl of a food processor, and puree. Measure out 2 tablespoons of the puree, and set aside.

Place the flour and the butter in a large bowl. Using a pastry cutter or two forks, quickly work the flour into the butter until it resembles coarse meal. Stir in 3 tablespoons of the Parmesan cheese, and the baking powder; add the egg, egg yolk, and asparagus puree, mixing just until a dough forms.

Remove the dough from the bowl and knead by hand until it comes together. Wrap well in plastic wrap and let rest, refrigerated, at least 15 minutes. At this point, the dough can be stored for up to 2 days.

On a lightly floured surface, roll the dough into a rectangle about $1/2$-inch thick, then cut into long strips, about $1/2$-inch wide each. Place on a lightly greased baking sheet and twist them slightly to form spiral. Bake, 5 to 7 minutes, until golden brown. Remove the pan from the oven and sprinkle the cheese straws with the remaining Parmesan cheese while they are still hot. Serve warm or at room temperature.

Wild Rice Stuffing with Sausage

BYRON J. BARDY, CMC, AAC, FOOD SERVICE CONSULTANT, PITTSBURGH, PA

Originally hand-harvested by Native Americans in canoes, wild rice originates from the aquatic grasses surrounding the Great Lakes. Its chewy texture and nutty, smoky flavor pair well with a soft, savory bread stuffing, and its indigenous roots lend a touch of tradition at Thanksgiving or any time of year.

MAKES 6 TO 8 SERVINGS

⅓ cup wild rice, dry

3 cups chicken stock

2 tablespoons pine nuts (pignoli)

½ pound sage sausage (plain pork
    sausage meat may be substituted;
    add 2 more sage leaves)

½ cup (1 stick) butter

2 celery stalks, diced

1 onion, diced

2 teaspoons freshly chopped parsley

1 teaspoon freshly chopped sage

Salt and freshly ground black pepper

1 pound loaf white bread, crusts removed,
    cut into ¾-inch cubes

To prepare the wild rice, combine the rice with 2 cups of the chicken stock in a small saucepan and bring to a boil. Cover, turn the heat to low, and cook for 50 minutes, or until the grains have puffed and are tender. Drain; transfer to a large bowl. The rice may be prepared up to a day in advance.

Preheat the oven to 325°F.

Place the pine nuts in a small, dry skillet set over medium heat, tossing occasionally, 4 to 5 minutes or until lightly toasted. Set aside.

Brown the sausage in a large skillet set over high heat, stirring to break it up; about 4 to 5 minutes, if the sausage is spread in an even layer. Using a slotted spoon, transfer the sausage to the bowl containing the rice. Drain off all but 1 tablespoon fat from the skillet, add 2 tablespoons of the butter, and place over medium heat. When the butter is melted and bubbly, add the celery, onion, parsley, and sage; season with salt and pepper. Cook, stirring, until the onion is translucent, about 5 minutes. Transfer the vegetables to the bowl with the rice and sausage, and place the pan back on the heat. Add the remaining cup of chicken broth and heat until simmering.

While the chicken broth warms, fold the bread cubes and pine nuts into the sausage-and-vegetable mixture. Pour the simmering stock into the bowl; stir well.

Lightly grease a glass or ceramic casserole with a teaspoon of the butter. Spoon the stuffing into the casserole, and smooth into an even layer. Dot the top with the remaining butter, cover tightly with foil, and bake for 1 hour and 45 minutes; uncover and bake another 15 minutes.

Obatzda
(Bavarian Cheese Dip)

LISA BREFERE, CEC, AAC, EXECUTIVE CHEF,
FLIK INTERNATIONAL AT BEAR STEARNS, NEW YORK, NY

At *brotzeit*, bread time, German friends and colleagues gather to discuss the day's events over beer and snacks. *Obatzda*, a traditional soft-cheese-and-beer dip from Bavaria, is still found on many beerhouse menus. Served with vegetables and bread, it is the perfect in-between-meal bite to accompany a great beer. When working with German-born chef Michael Schenk at a New York brewery, we introduced obatzda to our menu . . . it quickly became a favorite of our customers.

MAKES 8 SERVINGS

1 pound Brie or Camembert, coarsely chopped

6 ounces cream cheese

¼ cup (½ stick) butter, cut into small pieces

¼ cup dark German ale

3 cloves roasted garlic (see note)

1 teaspoon caraway seeds

Pinch sweet paprika

Salt and freshly ground black pepper

¼ cup diced Spanish onion

1 loaf French or German bread

⅓ cup thinly sliced red or Vidalia onion
    (for garnish)

¼ cup thinly sliced radishes (for garnish)

Cut vegetables, such as carrots or celery sticks,
    sliced bell peppers (green, red, and/or yellow),
    and bite-sized florets of broccoli and cauliflower

½ pound mixed olives

Place the Brie or Camembert in a medium bowl. Add the cream cheese, butter, ale, garlic, and caraway seeds. Add paprika, and salt and pepper to taste; beat well to combine.

In a strainer, rinse the diced onion under cold water. Drain and transfer to a clean kitchen towel, squeezing out all the liquid. Fold the onions into the cheese mixture. Cover and refrigerate, at least 2 hours, allowing the flavors to meld, or store, covered and refrigerated, for up to 4 days.

If using French bread, slice into ¼-inch-thick slices. If using German bread, halve lengthwise, then slice into ¼-inch-thick slices. To serve, top the obatzda with the Vidalia onion and radish slices, and surround with fresh cut vegetables, olives, and slices of French or German hard bread.

TO ROAST THE GARLIC:

Peel off any papery coating from the garlic head. Using a large, sharp knife, cut about ½ inch from the top of the bulb, exposing the tips of garlic cloves. Place in a small baking dish, drizzle lightly with olive oil, and season with salt. Pour ¼ cup of water in the bottom of the dish, cover tightly with foil, and roast in 375°F oven, about 1 hour. A sharp paring knife should insert into the garlic easily.

Saffron-Macadamia Nut Rice

STAFFORD T. DE CAMBRA, CEC, CCE, AAC, SENIOR EXECUTIVE CHEF,
S.S. INDEPENDENCE, AMERICAN HAWAII CRUISES

If you're tired of serving plain white rice, try this recipe with baked or grilled fish or a braised boneless chicken dish. It was created specifically for Asian Eggplant Curry (page 55).

MAKES 4 TO 6 SERVINGS

2 cups long-grain white rice

3¹/₂ cups chicken or vegetable stock

Two 2-inch pieces lemon grass, trimmed

¹/₂ cup chopped macadamia nuts

Pinch saffron, soaked in 1 tablespoon of water

2 tablespoons minced scallions

Salt and freshly ground black pepper

Place the rice in a sieve and rinse under cold water. In a medium saucepan, combine the rice with the stock and lemon grass, and bring to a boil. Reduce the heat to low; stir in the macadamia nuts and saffron. Cover and simmer until the rice is tender and has absorbed the liquid, about 20 minutes.

Add the scallions, season to taste, and stir briefly. Serve hot.

Savory Chestnut Custard

STEVE LA COUNT, CEC, AAC, EXECUTIVE CHEF,
THE COUNTRY CLUB, BROOKLINE, MA

The popularity of chestnuts in America dates back to Native Americans who made bread from chestnut flour. Although chestnut trees once dominated more than nine million acres of forests in the eastern United States, between 1900 and 1950, a lethal fungus reduced this once abundant crop to dead and dying stems. Today, botanists are working to cross-breed the American species with disease-hardy species from China to rebuild this important American crop.

This delicious and versatile chestnut custard may be served as a side dish to any kind of poultry, or even as a dessert, topped with maple syrup or maple ice cream.

MAKES 6 SERVINGS

2 teaspoons butter, softened

½ cup whole, canned chestnuts, drained

2 cups light cream

4 large egg yolks

Salt and ground white pepper

Preheat the oven to 350°F.

Lightly butter six 4-ounce ramekins. Set aside.

Roughly crush or chop the chestnuts; place half the pieces in a medium saucepan with the cream. Cook over medium heat until the mixture begins to steam; remove from heat, and set aside to steep for 10 minutes. Drain the cream into a medium bowl.

In a small bowl, beat the egg yolks. Stir in 2 tablespoons of the hot cream. Pour the tempered eggs into the bowl with the remaining cream, whisking constantly. Season the custard with salt and white pepper.

Place remaining chestnuts in the bottom of the prepared ramekins, and pour the custard over the top. Cover the ramekins with aluminum foil, transfer to a baking dish, and pour hot water into the pan halfway up the sides of the ramekins. Place the baking dish in the oven and cook for 25 minutes. Remove the aluminum foil and cook for 10 minutes more; the custard should be slightly firm and set. Serve warm. You can also make the custards in advance, refrigerate them, and reheat in the microwave, covered with plastic wrap, until just heated through.

Macaroni Soufflé

FRITZ SONNENSCHMIDT, CMC, AAC, CULINARY DEAN,
THE CULINARY INSTITUTE OF AMERICA, HYDE PARK, NY

I call this vegetarian dish a soufflé because the whipped egg whites make it a light and airy dish, although the texture will more closely resemble a soft frittata. Like so many American recipes, this combines the techniques and ingredients of various ethnic cuisines—Italian, French, German—to create an all-new dish. In place of half-and-half, you can substitute light or heavy cream, or even milk.

MAKES 4 SERVINGS

$^1/_2$ green bell pepper, seeded and julienned

2 tablespoons ground pecans
(use a food processor)

2 tablespoons freshly squeezed lemon juice

1 tablespoon chopped fresh thyme,
or 1 teaspoon dried

8 ounces extra-firm tofu, drained

2 tablespoons butter

2 medium tomatoes

6 ounces dry elbow macaroni or ziti

One 10-ounce box frozen peas

Salt and freshly ground black pepper

3 large eggs, separated

$^3/_4$ cup half-and-half

$^3/_4$ cup freshly grated Parmesan cheese

In a medium bowl, combine the pepper, pecans, lemon juice, and thyme. Cut the tofu into $^1/_2$-inch cubes, place in the bowl, and gently stir to combine. Marinate for 1 hour.

Preheat the oven to 400°F. Lightly grease a 1- to $1^1/_2$-quart casserole with 1 teaspoon of the butter. Set aside.

Bring a large pot of water to a boil. Add the tomatoes and cook until their skins loosen, 30 seconds to 1 minute. Using a slotted spoon remove the tomatoes, and transfer to a bowl to cool slightly. (Do not remove the pot of water from the heat.) Peel and discard the skins and dice the tomatoes. Set aside.

Salt the pot of boiling water, add the macaroni or ziti, and cook, stirring occasionally, 5 minutes. Drain; rinse under cold water. Drain again, and transfer to a large bowl.

Add the tomatoes, tofu, and peas to the pasta, season with salt and pepper, and stir gently. Lightly beat the egg yolk with half-and-half. Fold the egg mixture and the Parmesan cheese into the bowl with the tofu and macaroni. Set aside.

In the bowl of a standing mixer or using a hand-held mixer, beat the egg whites until soft peaks form. Fold the whites into the bowl. Transfer the contents to the prepared casserole. Dot the top with the remaining butter, and place the dish into the preheated oven. Bake until lightly browned, about 40 minutes.

Asian Eggplant Curry

STAFFORD T. DE CAMBRA, CEC, CCE, AAC, SENIOR EXECUTIVE CHEF,
S.S. INDEPENDENCE, AMERICAN HAWAII CRUISES

Chinatown in Hawaii is bustling on Saturdays. That is when the cruise ship I work on docks, and I have a chance to walk through the markets. Asian immigrants sell produce that they've transplanted from their homelands, and I can usually find small, purple Japanese eggplant, as well as the smaller and rounder, green Thai variety, for sale there. You can use any Asian eggplant in this recipe, but do not substitute the common Italian variety—it will get too mushy. This dish is good enough to eat with plain white rice or basmati rice, but it was created especially to be paired with Saffron Macadamia Nut Rice (page 52).

MAKES 6 SERVINGS

¹/₄ cup olive oil

2 tablespoons minced garlic

³/₄ cup diced Japanese eggplant

³/₄ cup diced Thai eggplant

1 cup diced zucchini

1 cup diced red bell pepper

1 tablespoon ground cumin

2 teaspoons ground turmeric

1 teaspoon curry powder

¹/₈ teaspoon hot red pepper flakes

¹/₈ teaspoon Thai curry paste (available in Asian markets)

1 cup mango chutney

1 cup cooked or canned, drained, chick peas (garbanzo beans)

2 cups dark raisins

1 cup unsweetened coconut flakes

¹/₄ cup chopped cilantro

Salt and freshly ground black pepper

6 cups hot cooked rice

6 tablespoons sliced scallions

Heat the olive oil in a large sauté pan over medium heat. Add the garlic, cook for 30 seconds, then add both kinds of eggplant, the zucchini, and the peppers. Cook, tossing or stirring, until tender, 5 to 7 minutes. Add the cumin, turmeric, curry, red pepper flakes, and Thai curry paste, stirring to blend; cook for a moment to toast the spices.

Add the chutney, chick peas, raisins and coconut flakes; cook, 3 to 4 minutes, to develop the flavors and moisten the raisins. Remove from the heat, stir in the cilantro, and adjust the seasoning with salt and pepper.

Place the eggplant curry on a bed of rice and sprinkle with scallions.

Turtle Bay Estate Potato Pancakes

HANS J. SCHADLER, CEC, AAC, EXECUTIVE CHEF,
CANEEL BAY RESORT, ST. JOHN, U.S. VIRGIN ISLANDS

Traditional potato pancakes, a favorite holiday dish also known as *latkes* to Jewish Americans, take on an island flair when served with slices of ripe guava and apples.

MAKES 4 TO 6 SERVINGS

FOR THE GUAVA APPLESAUCE:

1/4 cup (1/2 stick) butter

2 tablespoons dark-brown sugar

1 tablespoon honey

2 tablespoons freshly squeezed lemon juice

1/2 pound Granny Smith apples,
    cored and quartered

3 fresh guavas, peeled and quartered, or substitute
    2 tablespoons frozen guava puree, thawed
    (available in Spanish markets)

1/2 teaspoon ground cinnamon

1/2 teaspoon ground nutmeg

Pinch ground cloves

1/4 cup apple juice

2 tablespoons guava nectar, optional

FOR THE POTATO PANCAKES:

2 medium Yukon Gold potatoes
    (about 8 ounces total), halved lengthwise

1 medium or 2 small sweet potatoes
    (about 8 ounces total), halved lengthwise

1 small onion, grated

2 large eggs, lightly beaten

2 tablespoons all-purpose flour

2 tablespoons apple juice

1 tablespoon freshly squeezed lemon juice

2 tablespoons fresh chopped chives

Pinch ground nutmeg

Pinch sugar

Salt and freshly ground black pepper

1/4 cup olive oil

TO MAKE THE GUAVA APPLESAUCE:

In a sauté pan over medium heat, melt the butter. Add the brown sugar and cook, stirring, to lightly caramelize the sugar, 2 to 3 minutes.

Add the honey and lemon juice, and stir. Add the apples and guavas (or guava puree) and cook, stirring, 5 minutes, to soften the fruit. Add the spices, apple juice, and guava nectar, stir well, and cover. Bring the mixture to a boil, reduce the heat, and simmer for about 30 minutes. Press the mixture through a food mill or fine chinoise; adjust the seasonings to taste.

TO MAKE THE POTATO PANCAKES:

Place the potato and sweet-potato halves in a medium saucepan, cover with water, and bring to a boil. Lower the heat to gently boil and cook, 8 to 10 minutes, until the potatoes are slightly underdone. There should be slight resistance when a thin-bladed knife is inserted into the potato. Drain, let cool slightly, then peel and grate the potatoes.

Place the grated potatoes and the onion in the center of a clean dishtowel; gently squeeze out any excess liquid. Transfer to a large bowl and add the eggs, flour, apple and lemon juice, and the chives; season with nutmeg, sugar, and salt and pepper. Using a rubber spatula, gently fold the ingredients together. Using your hands, form 6 medium or 4 large patties.

Heat the olive oil in a large nonstick skillet over medium heat. When the oil is wavy, add the potato patties and cook until golden brown and crispy on both sides, about 2 to 3 minutes per side. Drain on paper towels. Serve the potato pancakes while still hot, with the guava applesauce on the side.

CHAPTER THREE

Poultry

Simple or Elegant, A Versatile
Favorite of American Cuisine

W HILE TRADITIONALLY, AMERICA HAS BEEN viewed as a nation of meat-and-potato eaters, today it is poultry that is the main course of choice. Once expensive and considered a luxury food (hence its relegation to Sunday dinners), poultry, particularly chicken, is now a ubiquitous and versatile part of the American culinary landscape.

Chicken didn't always enjoy this popularity as a food item. In fact, these birds were once viewed as being of greater value for their eggs than their meat, and were only eaten after their productive days had come to an end. Chicken Fricassee utilizes a slow-cooking method that was used by thrifty farmers to transform tough, older chickens into a tender, tasty main dish. For the grill, try the Char-Grilled Chicken Breasts with Indian-Summer Sweet Corn and Chili-Pepper Relish, which uses farm-stand ingredients of late summer, or the Grilled Chicken with

Caribbean Salsa, flavored with zesty jerk seasonings. The Raspberry Chicken Breast with Spinach and Feta Stuffing was inspired by the cuisines of the Italian and Greek communities of New England, while the Crispy Sesame Chicken Satay with Pico de Gallo is yet another example of the delicious things that can happen when two cuisines come together on the same plate.

Chicken, however, is not the only poultry making its mark in American cuisine. Turkey, once relegated to the traditional holiday table, appears today in new forms in our supermarkets and on our tables—the Pilsner-Infused Flamed Turkey Steaks make use of the now widely-available turkey cutlet; and the Stuffed Cornish Game Hen with Apple Cider Glaze, Cinnamon Apple Roasted Duck, and Sautéed Breast of Duck with Cranberry Compote all make use of native American ingredients to create satisfying poultry dishes that reflect new American tastes.

Char-Grilled Chicken Breasts with Indian-Summer Sweet Corn and Chile Pepper Relish

ANDREW G. IANNACCHIONE, CEC, AAC, OWNER, HOSPITALITY REFERRALS/CONSULTANTS, CORPORATE CONSULTING CHEF, U.S. FOODSERVICE, BEDFORD, PA

In most areas of America, the Indian summer—late summer and early fall—harvest is the most rewarding. Sweet corn is among the ingredients worth waiting for. This relish is a terrific side dish to grilled foods—try it with grilled shrimp too. With the hot sauce and chile peppers called for in the recipe, add just enough to suit your own personal tastes. I like to use habaneros, but serranos or jalapeños may be more appropriate.

MAKES 6 SERVINGS

FOR THE RELISH:

2 cups sweet corn cut from the cob (3 to 4 ears)

1/4 cup diced red onion

1/4 cup diced Spanish onion

1 cup peeled and diced cucumber

1/3 cup finely diced red pepper

1/3 cup finely diced green pepper

Juice of 1 lime

Salt and freshly ground black pepper

1 teaspoon hot sauce, or to taste

1 1/2 teaspoons ground cumin

1 1/2 teaspoons sugar

1/4 cup balsamic vinegar

1/4 cup extra-virgin olive oil

1/4 to 1/2 teaspoon seeded and minced hot chile pepper (use a variety of green and red chiles, if possible)

1 teaspoon minced garlic

FOR THE CHICKEN:

Six 8-ounce boneless, skinless chicken breasts

2 tablespoons olive oil

Salt and freshly ground black pepper

In a large bowl, combine the relish ingredients. Toss to combine. Cover and refrigerate at least 24 hours.

To prepare the chicken, preheat the grill. Rub the chicken breasts with the olive oil, season with salt and pepper, and place on the grill. Cook 6 to 8 minutes per side, until slightly charred and cooked through. Serve the chicken breasts topped with a generous spoonful of the relish.

Raspberry Chicken Breast with Spinach and Feta Stuffing

GINO A. CORELLI, CEC, AAC, EXECUTIVE CHEF,
BROWN UNIVERSITY FOOD SERVICE, PROVIDENCE, RI

New England's significant immigrant population includes both Italians and Greeks, who, in the early twentieth century, often lived side by side in the same communities. This recipe is a creation of my own, symbolic of that commingling of cultures—an Italian-style preparation made with favorite Greek ingredients, spinach and feta cheese.

MAKES 6 SERVINGS

6 boneless, skinless chicken breasts
   (7 to 8 ounces each)

⅓ cup raspberry vinegar

One 10-ounce box frozen chopped spinach

1½ tablespoons minced shallots

1 tablespoon butter

1 cup crumbled feta cheese (5 ounces)

1 large egg, lightly beaten

2 tablespoons Madeira wine

1 tablespoon chopped fresh dill

¼ teaspoon freshly ground black pepper

Place the chicken breasts in a shallow casserole or nonreactive baking pan, pour the raspberry vinegar over top, and turn the breasts to coat evenly. Cover and refrigerate, at least 45 minutes. Drain the vinegar and reserve. Form a pocket in each chicken breast, cutting lengthwise into, but not all the way through, the breast, about 2 inches. Set aside.

Preheat the oven to 375°F.

While the chicken breasts marinate, thaw the spinach and squeeze out any excess liquid. Set aside.

In a medium skillet, heat the butter over medium heat. When melted, add the shallots and cook, stirring, until translucent, 2 to 3 minutes. Add the spinach and cook, stirring often, another 3 to 4 minutes. Add the feta, egg, Madeira, dill, and pepper, mix well, and continue to cook, stirring, until the egg is set, 1 to 2 minutes. Remove from the heat and set aside to cool.

Place 2 to 3 tablespoons of the spinach-and-feta mixture into the pocket of each chicken breast. Arrange the chicken breasts, seam side down, in a shallow roasting pan and pour the reserved vinegar over the top. Place in the oven and cook, 25 to 30 minutes, or until the chicken breasts are cooked through.

Grilled Chicken with Caribbean Salsa

BYRON J. BARDY, CMC, AAC, FOOD SERVICE CONSULTANT, PITTSBURGH, PA

Classic *salsa fresca* is little more than chopped tomatoes, mixed with onion, garlic, and cilantro, best served with tortilla chips. During the last decade, salsa has grown tremendously in popularity; many of the delicious variations bear little resemblance to the original. The island-style salsa in this recipe is good enough to serve as a dip, but is even better over grilled chicken.

MAKES 4 SERVINGS

FOR THE CARIBBEAN SALSA:

2 cups diced fresh tomatoes

$1/2$ cup tomato juice

$1/4$ cup diced red onion

$1/4$ cup diced green Anaheim chile peppers (2 teaspoons minced jalapeño pepper may be substituted)

$1/4$ cup diced red bell pepper

$1/4$ cup diced yellow bell pepper

2 tablespoons fresh chopped cilantro

2 teaspoons favorite jerk seasoning

1 teaspoon freshly squeezed lime juice

1 teaspoon olive oil

Salt

FOR THE GRILLED CHICKEN:

4 chicken breast halves (about 6 ounces each)

1 tablespoon olive oil

Salt and freshly ground black pepper

TO PREPARE THE SALSA:

Combine all the ingredients in a medium bowl. Season with salt to taste, and toss or stir to incorporate. Cover and refrigerate for 2 to 3 hours before serving.

TO PREPARE THE CHICKEN:

Preheat the grill. Rub the chicken breast halves with olive oil and season with salt and pepper. Place them on the grill and cook, turning once, until well browned and cooked through, about 5 to 6 minutes per side. Serve topped with salsa.

Chicken Fricassee

KLAUS MULLER, CCE, AAC, DEAN, ACADEMY OF CULINARY ARTS, ATLANTIC CAPE COMMUNITY COLLEGE, MAYS LANDING, NJ

Chickens were once raised for their eggs, and weren't eaten until they were old and no longer productive. That meant the meat was dry and tough, so moist-cooking methods like braising, stewing, and fricasseeing were created to tenderize it. Today, in America, chickens are bred specifically for their meat, but I'm sure that you'll still enjoy this classic dish.

MAKES 4 SERVINGS

1/4 cup vegetable oil

1 onion, sliced

1 bay leaf

1 fryer chicken (3 to 4 pounds), excess skin and fat trimmed

Salt and freshly ground black pepper

3/4 cup all-purpose flour

1/2 cup white wine, such as Riesling

1 1/2 cups chicken stock

1 fresh thyme sprig

4 white button mushroom caps

1 large egg yolk

1/2 cup heavy cream

Heat 2 tablespoons of the oil in a braising pan over medium heat. Add the onion and bay leaf and cook, stirring, for about 5 minutes. Season the chicken with salt and pepper. Dredge in all but 2 tablespoons of the flour, shaking off the excess. Place the chicken on top of the onions; cook for a few minutes on each side. Do not brown.

Remove the chicken, add 1/3 cup of the white wine to the pan, stir, and reduce until almost complete evaporated. Add the 2 tablespoons reserved flour to the pan, stirring to blend. Add the chicken stock, thyme, and remaining white wine, and bring to a boil. Reduce the heat to a simmer, and return the chicken to the pan along with the mushroom caps. Cover and simmer, turning the chicken occasionally, until it is cooked, about 50 minutes.

Transfer the chicken and the mushrooms to a serving platter with sides. Beat egg yolk with the cream. Whisk the egg-cream mixture into the simmering cooking liquid and cook, stirring, for 1 minute. Strain the sauce, adjust the seasoning with salt and pepper, and spoon over the chicken.

Peach Tree Chicken

DOUGLAS J. POLMANN, CEC, AAC, EXECUTIVE CHEF,
OAK LANE COUNTRY CLUB, WOODBRIDGE, CT

Peach County, Georgia is known as the Peach Capital of the World. If you need more convincing that Georgians know their peaches, be sure to visit the Peach Festival held every June in Byron and Fort Valley. This recipe is a wonderful way to enjoy peaches all year long. Normally, I'm not a big fan of canned peaches, but the addition of peach schnapps really improves their flavor. I enjoy cooking with fruit-flavored liquors, because they can turn an otherwise ordinary dish into something special.

MAKES 4 SERVINGS

1/4 cup sun-dried tomatoes (not oil-soaked)

8 boneless, skinless chicken breast halves
    (3 to 4 ounces each)

1/4 cup (1/2 stick) butter

Salt and freshly ground black pepper

1 1/2 cups all-purpose flour

1/2 cup Peachtree peach schnapps

1/4 cup orange marmalade

8 canned peach halves, sliced, juice reserved

6 cinnamon sticks

1/2 cup orange juice

2 tablespoons cornstarch mixed with
    1/4 cup cold water

3 scallions, chopped, green part only

Preheat the oven to 350°F. Place the sun-dried tomatoes in a cup of hot water and set aside for at least 15 minutes to soften.

Pound the chicken breasts between 2 sheets of plastic wrap, one at a time, to about 1/4-inch thickness; try not to tear them.

Heat the butter in a large sauté pan over medium-high heat. Season the pounded breasts with salt and pepper, dredge them in flour, and shake off the excess. Place the chicken breasts into the pan and cook until golden brown on both sides, about 5 minutes. Transfer the cutlets to a baking dish large enough to hold them in one layer.

In a small saucepan, combine the schnapps and the marmalade. Stir, add the sliced peaches, and place over medium-high heat. Allow the mixture to boil until the fragrance of alcohol is gone, 2 to 3 minutes. Add the cinnamon sticks, orange juice, and the reserved peach juice. Bring to a boil and stir in the cornstarch mixture. Cook, stirring, until thickened, about 2 minutes. Remove the sun-dried tomatoes from the water and cut into thin strips. Stir in the sun-dried tomatoes, adjust the seasoning, and spoon the sauce over the chicken. Place the pan in the oven and roast for 5 minutes. Transfer the chicken cutlets to serving plates, spoon the sauce over it, and sprinkle with the scallions.

Umbrella Chicken

HARRY BROCKWELL, CEC, AAC, OCEANSIDE CATERERS, WESTLAKE VILLAGE, CA

My catering business gets a lot of requests for luaus and Pacific-Rim-themed parties, and this Chinese-style dish is always a favorite. I love it because it can be prepared far in advance, and refrigerated or frozen, then fried at the very last minute for a fresh taste and crispy texture. The drumette, the meaty part of a chicken wing, makes excellent finger food, especially when the chicken is scraped to one end, leaving a neat umbrella shape. You may need to buy whole wings; if so, cut them at the joint to get the drumettes, and save the remaining wing portions for stock.

MAKES 4 SERVINGS

1¼ pounds chicken drumettes

6 tablespoons soy sauce

10 tablespoons dark brown sugar

½ cup dry sherry

1 tablespoon white-wine vinegar

1 cup all-purpose flour

Vegetable oil for deep frying

Salt

Using a small sharp knife, cut around the bone at the small end of each drumette to release the meat. Scrape the chicken upward along the bone to form a fat lump of meat at the other end. Place the chicken into a small baking pan with sides and set aside.

In a small bowl, prepare the marinade. Combine 4 tablespoons of the soy sauce with 5½ tablespoons of the brown sugar, and the sherry. Whisk the mixture together then pour over the chicken pieces, shaking the pan to evenly coat the drumettes with the marinade. Cover and refrigerate at least 3 hours.

Meanwhile, prepare the dipping sauce. In a small saucepan, whisk the remaining 2 tablespoons soy sauce, remaining 4½ tablespoons brown sugar, and the vinegar and place over medium heat. Bring the mixture to a boil, stirring often. Remove from the heat and transfer to a small serving bowl.

Preheat the oven to 375°F.

Prepare a steamer with simmering water. Spread the flour in a medium, shallow bowl. Remove the drumettes from the marinade, drain, and roll them in the flour. Shake off any excess and add the drumettes to the steamer basket, standing them on end, meat end down. Place the steamer basket in the steamer and cook for about 25 minutes. The drumettes may be prepared in advance to this point, then refrigerated or frozen.

Place the oil in a heavy Dutch oven or fryer to a depth of 1½ inches and place over medium-high heat, bringing the oil to 350°F. Add half the chicken drumettes and cook until cooked through and golden, about 3 minutes. Transfer them to a paper towel-lined plate or baking pan, season with salt, and repeat with the remaining drumettes, adding more oil if necessary. Serve immediately, on a platter, with the dipping sauce in the center.

Breast of Chicken Valle Verde

ELIZABETH B. MIKESELL, CEC, AAC, AND WILLARD SPRINGER,
THE COUNTRY CLUB OF GREEN VALLEY, AZ

Southwestern desert cooking showcases the many influences of neighboring Mexico. In this recipe the citrus, chile, and cilantro marinade tenderize and infuse flavor into the chicken breasts. If this recipe seems daunting, try substituting store-bought tortilla chips for fried tortilla. If possible, purchase tortilla strips for a more decorative touch.

MAKES 6 SERVINGS

FOR THE MARINADE:

10 crushed and peeled cloves garlic

2 chipotle chiles, minced

Grated zest and juice of 1 lime

Grated zest and juice of 1 orange

1 bunch cilantro, finely chopped

1/4 cup corn oil

1/2 teaspoon salt

6 boneless, skinless chicken breasts
    (5 to 6 ounces each)

FOR THE SAUCE:

6 tablespoons tequila

4 cloves garlic, minced

2 chipotle chiles, minced

2 tablespoons prickly pear preserve or jam
    (with or without seeds; red currant jelly
    may be substituted)

Grated zest and juice of 2 oranges

Grated zest and juice of 1 lime

1 cup heavy cream

1/2 teaspoon salt

6 corn tortillas, cut into strips

Corn oil, as needed, to fry tortillas

3 poblano chiles

8 ounces goat cheese, cut into 4 disks

Prepare the marinade, whisking together all the ingredients in a small bowl. Place the chicken breasts in one layer in a baking dish or a nonreactive container with sides. Pour the marinade over the chicken and turn to coat evenly. Cover and refrigerate for at least 2 hours.

Prepare the sauce, combining all the sauce ingredients in a small saucepan. Stir well, and bring to a boil, then reduce the heat, and maintain a low boil until the liquid is reduced by half.

While the sauce reduces, fry the tortilla strips. Heat 2 inches of the corn oil in a medium skillet. When the oil is wavy (375°F), add the tortilla strips and cook, turning or moving with a fork, until lightly browned and crispy, 1 to 2 minutes. Using a skimmer, transfer the tortilla strips to a paper towel-lined plate. When the sauce is reduced, add a small handful of the fried tortilla strips and cook until they just soften and thicken the sauce, about 1 minute. Remove the sauce from the heat and keep warm.

Preheat the broiler. To peel the poblano peppers, place them in a small roasting pan under the broiler about 4 to 5 inches from the heat source. Cook, turning the peppers often, until evenly blistered and lightly charred. Transfer to a bowl and cover with plastic. When cool enough to handle, peel, discarding skins, seeds, and stems. Cut into thin strips. Set aside. Keep the broiler hot.

Wipe excess marinade from the chicken breasts and place them in a single layer on a broiling or shallow roasting pan. Broil the chicken, turning once or twice, until evenly browned and cooked through, about 6 minutes per side. Remove from the heat and slice each breast into 3 to 4 slices on the diagonal. Place the slices on serving plates and top with a spoonful of sauce, a piece of goat cheese, and strips of the poblano chiles and fried tortillas.

Crispy Sesame Chicken Satay with Pico de Gallo

RUDY GARCIA, CEC, AAC, EXECUTIVE CHEF, CULINARY ARTS,
LOS ANGELES MISSION COLLEGE, LOS ANGELES, CA

Southern California has significant Mexican and Asian populations, and this recipe reflects this cultural blend, bringing together diverse flavors in a deliciously unique way. The chicken and vegetables are prepared with Asian ingredients like sesame oil, peanut oil, and fresh ginger, then served with traditional Mexican *pico de gallo*. I prefer *pico de gallo* on the spicy side, but you can reduce the amount of chile to taste.

MAKES 8 SERVINGS

FOR THE PICO DE GALLO:

4 tomatoes, diced

1 to 2 tablespoons minced serrano chile, or to taste

1/2 cup chopped cilantro (about 1 large bunch)

1 onion, finely diced

1 tablespoon minced garlic

Juice of 1 lemon

Juice of 1 lime

Salt and freshly ground white pepper

FOR THE SESAME CHICKEN:

8 boneless, skinless chicken breasts

2 tablespoons sesame oil

1 red bell pepper, cored, seeded and cut into thin strips

1 green bell pepper, cored, seeded and cut into thin strips

1/2 cup fresh chopped cilantro (about 1 large bunch)

1 tablespoon minced fresh ginger

Salt and freshly ground white pepper

2 tablespoons peanut oil

1/4 cup black sesame seeds (regular sesame seeds may be substituted)

1/4 cup cornstarch

TO PREPARE THE PICO DE GALLO:

Combine all the ingredients in a medium bowl; season with salt and white pepper. Set aside.

TO PREPARE THE CHICKEN:

Rub the chicken breasts with the sesame oil. Set aside.

In a large bowl, combine the red and green peppers, cilantro, and ginger; season with salt and pepper. Using your hands, mix the ingredients, rubbing gently to mix the flavors.

Heat the peanut oil in an oven-safe sauté pan or skillet over medium-high heat. Meanwhile, spread the sesame seeds on one plate and the cornstarch on another. Press the chicken breasts into the sesame seeds, lightly coating, then into the cornstarch, shaking off the excess. Place the chicken breasts into the pan, increase the heat to high, and brown the chicken breasts on both sides, 2 to 3 minutes per side. Transfer the pan to the oven and cook for 20 minutes, or until cooked through. Remove the chicken from the pan; and return the pan to the stove.

Add the vegetables to the pan and cook over medium heat, stirring, until transparent, 2 to 3 minutes. Return the chicken to the pan until just heated, then transfer the chicken and vegetables to serving plates. Top with the *pico de gallo* and serve.

Sesame Chicken with Northern White Bean Ragout

JOHN R. FISHER, CEC, AAC, ACADEMIC DEPARTMENT DIRECTOR CULINARY ARTS, THE ART INSTITUTE OF SEATTLE, SEATTLE, WA

This dish represents Pan-Asian Pacific Rim cooking with a Northwestern accent. I use free-range Washington State chicken breasts, but any flavorful variety will do. The Skagit Valley is well known for its abundance of root vegetables, such as carrots, turnips, rutabagas, and parsnips, which lend themselves to country-style cooking—that's where my inspiration for this hearty white bean ragout came from. Try this with the Basil Pesto Spinach Timbale (page 40), a soft and savory contrast to this dish.

MAKES 6 SERVINGS

FOR THE SESAME CHICKEN:

1/4 cup reduced-sodium soy sauce

1/4 cup orange juice

1/4 cup dry white wine

1/4 cup honey

1/4 cup ketchup

2 tablespoons sesame oil

1 tablespoon minced fresh ginger

1 tablespoon fresh chopped cilantro

Salt and freshly ground pepper

2 pounds boneless, skinless chicken breasts, cut into 2-inch chunks

FOR THE NORTHERN WHITE BEAN RAGOUT:

2 cups dried Northern White beans (soaked overnight)

1 tablespoon butter

1 small onion, diced

1 carrot, peeled and diced

1 celery stalk, diced

1 garlic clove, crushed

2 cups chicken stock

2 cups veal stock, or 2 additional cups chicken stock

1 bay leaf

1 medium tomato, chopped

1 tablespoon apple cider vinegar

1 tablespoon chopped flat-leaf parsley

TO PREPARE THE CHICKEN:

In a large bowl, stir together all the sesame chicken ingredients, except for the chicken. When the mixture is well combined, fold in the chicken, evenly coating each piece with the marinade. Cover and refrigerate, at least 8 hours.

Preheat the oven to 350°F.

TO PREPARE THE NORTHERN WHITE BEAN RAGOUT:

In a medium oven-safe saucepan, heat the butter over medium heat. When bubbling, add the onion, carrot, celery, and garlic and cook, stirring, until the vegetables soften, about 5 minutes. Add the beans, chicken stock, veal stock (if using), and bay leaf. Bring to a boil, then cover and transfer to the oven. Cook for 50 minutes or until the beans are tender; add a little liquid if the beans look dry while cooking. Stir in the tomato, cider vinegar, and parsley and keep warm. Keep the oven set at 350°F.

TO COMPLETE THE DISH:

Preheat the grill. Thread the chicken pieces onto 6 skewers and place on the grill rack. Cook, turning often, until the chicken is cooked through, 6 to 8 minutes.

To serve, place the beans in the center of each serving plate and top with a chicken skewer.

Chicken á la Chinita

BOB BURNS, CEC, AAC, EXECUTIVE CHEF,
COLUMBUS COUNTRY CLUB, COLUMBUS, OH

When traveling around the world, I find that the easiest way to break down cultural and political barriers is by talking about food. Throughout Latin and South America, there are very large populations of Asians, particularly Japanese and Chinese, in countries like Brazil, Chile and Peru. In fact, Lima has one of the largest Chinatowns in the world, and the Prime Minister of Peru has for the last several years been of Japanese descent. This recipe is a prime example of how these cultures interact, through food—traditional Spanish ingredients like cumin and chile peppers are combined with scallions and fresh ginger, and stir-fried in the Chinese manner.

MAKES 4 SERVINGS

2 pounds boneless, skinless chicken breasts

2 tablespoons dry sherry

1 tablespoon coarse salt

2 teaspoons balsamic vinegar

1 teaspoon turmeric

1 teaspoon ground cumin

3 large cloves garlic, crushed

4 tablespoons vegetable oil

1 large green bell pepper, julienned

2 large yellow bell peppers, julienned

3 large red bell peppers, julienned

1 jalapeño pepper, seeded and minced

4 carrots, peeled and julienned

1 tablespoon minced fresh ginger

8 scallions, cut in 2-inch segments

3/4 pound sugar-snap peas, ends trimmed

1/4 cup chopped roasted peanuts

2 tablespoons chopped fresh thyme
   (if using dried, use 2 teaspoons, and add it
   along with the garlic to make the paste)

2 cups cooked white rice

Slice the chicken breasts into 1/4-inch-wide strips. Place in a large bowl and set aside.

In the bowl of a mini-food processor fitted with the metal blade, or by hand using a mortar and pestle, process the sherry, coarse salt, balsamic vinegar, turmeric, cumin, and 1 garlic clove. Add this paste to the chicken strips, rubbing with your hands to evenly coat. Set aside.

Heat 2 tablespoons of the oil and the remaining garlic in a large wok or sauté pan over medium-high heat. Cook, stirring, until the garlic is golden brown, then strain the garlic from the wok or pan and discard. Add the chicken to the wok and cook, stirring, until it is no longer pink, 2 to 3 minutes. Transfer to a plate, loosely cover, and set aside.

Heat the remaining 2 tablespoons oil in the wok, and add the bell and jalapeño peppers, carrots, and ginger. Cook, stirring, for 10 seconds, then add the scallions and snap peas. Cook, stirring frequently, for 2 minutes. Add the chicken, peanuts, and thyme, and cook another 1 to 2 minutes.

Portion 1/2 cup rice onto each plate and top with the chicken and vegetables.

Jersey Shore Grilled Chicken, Tomato, and Crab

THOMAS BIGLAN, CEC, AAC, VICE PRESIDENT, FOOD AND BEVERAGE SERVICES, SANDS CASINO HOTEL, ATLANTIC CITY, NJ

New Jersey tomatoes are recognized nationwide for their exceptional size, taste and intense color. During the peak harvest, from July through September, chefs and home cooks use them in salads, soups, sauces, and entrees. At the Jersey Shore, this dish, marrying New Jersey tomatoes with succulent local crabs, is a traditional favorite among shore residents and tourists alike.

MAKES 6 SERVINGS

½ cup olive oil

1 tablespoon chopped fresh parsley

1 teaspoon chopped fresh sage

½ teaspoon Old Bay Seasoning

Salt and freshly ground black pepper

6 boneless, skinless chicken breasts (about 5 ounces each)

3 Jersey tomatoes

2 tablespoons butter

1 teaspoon minced shallots

2 tablespoons dry white wine

2 cups half & half or light cream

1 ounce Gorgonzola cheese, crumbled

¼ cup freshly grated Parmesan cheese

2 ounces provolone cheese, diced

2 ounces fontina cheese, diced

½ cup seasoned breadcrumbs

12 ounces jumbo lump crabmeat, picked over

6 basil leaves, cut into long ribbons

In a small bowl, whisk the olive oil, parsley, sage, and Old Bay Seasoning; season with salt and pepper.

Place the chicken breasts into a large shallow bowl or baking dish and pour the marinade over top, turning the chicken pieces to evenly coat. Cover and refrigerate at least 30 minutes.

Preheat the grill. Preheat the oven to 250°F.

Cut the center core from the tomatoes and slice 4 thick slices from the center, leaving the two rounded ends, which should be diced. Set aside.

Heat 1 tablespoon of the butter in a medium saucepan over medium heat. Add the shallots and cook, stirring, 2 minutes. Add the diced tomato, cook another minute, then stir in the white wine. When the white wine is almost completely reduced, stir in the half & half and the cheeses. Heat just to a boil, reduce the heat and simmer slowly, stirring constantly, until the sauce is creamy and thick enough to coat the back of a spoon, 2 to 3 minutes. Strain the sauce, then set aside and keep warm.

Spread the breadcrumbs on a plate. Press the tomato slices into breadcrumbs, coating each side. Place the tomato slices onto the hot grill and cook until lightly browned, about 2 minutes per side. Transfer to a platter and loosely cover to keep warm.

Remove the chicken breasts from the marinade, wiping off any excess. Place them on the grill, and cook, turning after 4 to 5 minutes, until cooked through, 10 to 12 minutes total. Transfer the cooked chicken to a platter and place in the oven to keep warm.

In a medium skillet, heat the remaining butter over medium-high heat. Add the crabmeat and cook, stirring, for about 5 minutes; season with salt and pepper.

To serve, place a chicken breast on each serving plate and top with a tomato slice, a spoonful of the crabmeat, and top with the cheese sauce. Garnish with the basil and serve.

PREPARING BONELESS, SKINLESS CHICKEN BREASTS

While boneless, skinless chicken breasts are readily available, it is much more economical to purchase whole breasts with the bone still attached and debone them yourself. Following is the method:

1. Make a cut along one side of the breastbone to free the breast from the rib cage (Fig. 1).

2. Pull the meat away from the bones as the cut is made so that as little meat as possible is left on the bones (Fig. 2).

3. Make a cut through the joint that attaches the wing to the rib cage and remove the wing (Fig. 3).

4. Carefully pull the layer of skin away from the breast meat, and the process is complete (Fig. 4).

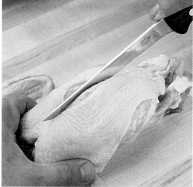
1.

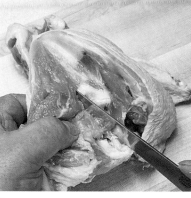
2.

3.

4.

Stuffed Cornish Game Hen with Apple Cider Glaze

VINCENT ALBERICI, AAC, EXECUTIVE CHEF,
ADAM'S MARK HOTEL, PHILADELPHIA, PA

This easy, home-style recipe for Cornish game hen is perfect for anyone who is tired of serving the same old chicken dishes night after night. Try it when the weather turns cool in the fall, and fresh apple cider appears at the local farmer's market. The hazelnuts add an unexpected twist to traditional bread stuffing, but almonds can be used as well.

MAKES 6 SERVINGS

FOR THE CORNISH GAME HEN:

1 tablespoon butter

2 heaping tablespoons minced onion

1 tablespoon minced garlic

$3/4$ cup diced white button mushrooms

1 cup diced stale bread

$1/3$ cup chopped, toasted hazelnuts (see note)

$1/3$ cup diced dried apricots

$3/4$ tablespoon fresh thyme, chopped,
    or a pinch of dried

$3/4$ tablespoon fresh oregano, chopped,
    or a pinch of dried

2 tablespoons chopped flat-leaf parsley

1 large egg

$1/4$ cup milk

Salt and freshly ground black pepper

6 Cornish game hens (about $1^1/4$ pounds each),
    rinsed and patted dry

TO PREPARE THE CORNISH GAME HENS:

Preheat the oven to 375°F.

Heat the butter in a large sauté pan over medium-high heat. Add the onion and garlic and cook, stirring, for 1 minute. Add the mushrooms and cook, stirring, for another minute. Remove from the heat and let the mushroom mixture cool.

In a mixing bowl, combine the cooled mushroom mixture with the remaining Cornish hen ingredients. Stuff the mixture into the cavity of the hens, place the hens on a roasting rack, and season with salt and pepper.

Place the rack in a roasting pan and transfer to the oven. Cook for about 45 minutes, or until the juices run clear when the thigh is pierced with a knife.

(recipe continues on p.78)

TO TOAST THE HAZELNUTS:

Place the hazelnuts in a small skillet over medium heat. Cook, stirring occasionally, until lightly browned and fragrant, about 5 minutes.

Stuffed Cornish Game Hen with Apple Cider Glaze (continued)

1 tablespoon olive oil

1 tablespoon minced shallots

1 teaspoon minced fresh ginger,
    or ½ teaspoon ground ginger

¼ cup Chardonnay wine

⅓ cup apple cider

1 tablespoon cider vinegar

⅓ cup orange juice

1½ cups chicken stock

1 tablespoon honey

1 tablespoon chopped fresh tarragon leaves

Salt and freshly ground black pepper

TO PREPARE THE APPLE CIDER GLAZE:

Heat the olive oil in a small saucepan over medium-high heat. Add the shallots and ginger and cook, stirring, for 30 seconds. Add the Chardonnay, apple cider, cider vinegar, and orange juice; bring to a boil. Reduce the heat and simmer until the liquid is reduced by half, about 2 minutes. Add the chicken stock and honey and cook for another 3 minutes. Add the tarragon, and salt and pepper to taste.

TO COMPLETE THE DISH:

Remove the Cornish hens from the oven and let cool for 5 minutes. Remove the stuffing from the cavities. Reheat the glaze if necessary. Place stuffing alongside hen. Pour some of the apple cider glaze on top and serve.

QUARTERING A WHOLE BIRD

Whole birds frequently are halved or quartered in preparation for grilling or roasting. Often the bird is cut up further into eighths for frying, braising, or stewing, where the smaller pieces will cook more evenly. While cut-up birds are available from your supermarket or butcher, cutting up a whole bird yourself is simple and more economical:

1. Lay the bird on one side. Make a cut along one side of the backbone, working from the neck to the tail (Fig. 1).Turn the bird onto its other side and make a cut alont the other side of the backbone, this time from tail to neck.

2. Open the bird out flat, with the skin side facing down, Make a cut through the breast on one side of the keel bone to separate the bird into halves (Fig. 2).

3. Pull the keel bone away from the bird completely, being sure that none of it is left behind (Fig. 3). Complete the cut down the center of the breast to separate the two halves.

4. Make a diagonal cut across each of the two halves to separate the breast from the leg (Fig. 4).

5. The quartered bird (Fig. 5).

6. To cut the bird into eighths, make further cuts to separate the drumsticks from the thighs and the breasts from the wings (Fig. 6).

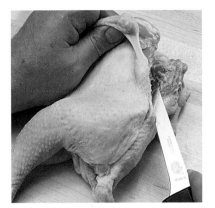

1.

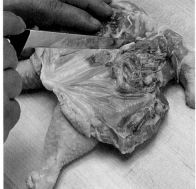

2.

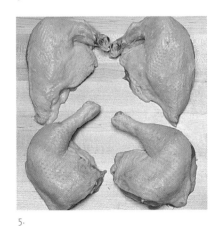

3.

4.

5.

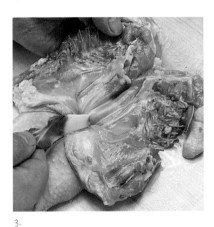

6.

Chicken Roulades

DOUGLAS J. POLMANN, CEC, AAC, EXECUTIVE CHEF,
OAK LANE COUNTRY CLUB, WOODBRIDGE, CT

The roulade is a concept that exists in countless forms in many cuisines, from the traditional Italian rolled and tied beef *braciole,* to light but sweet jelly-roll desserts. Though this recipe can be made with veal cutlets, I thought that a chicken roulade would be a welcome twist. In fact, it's one of my catering company's most popular dishes. Make this dish in the spring when asparagus is at its best.

MAKES 4 SERVINGS

1/2 cup (1 stick) butter

4 red bell peppers, halved and seeded

Salt

16 asparagus spears

3 portobello mushroom caps, sliced

Eight 4-ounce boneless, skinless, chicken cutlets

Freshly ground black pepper

8 slices provolone or mozzarella cheese

1 cup all-purpose flour

1/2 cup Chardonnay wine

1 1/2 cups favorite prepared brown sauce or gravy

Preheat the broiler.

Soften 1 tablespoon of the butter and rub it over the pepper halves. Place the pepper halves in 1 layer on a sheet pan, and set under the broiler. Cook, turning once, until blistered and lightly charred, about 5 minutes. Transfer the peppers to a bowl and cover tightly with plastic wrap. When the peppers are cool enough to handle, peel and discard the skins. Set the roasted pepper halves aside. Turn oven temperature to 350°F.

Bring a medium saucepan of water to a boil. Season generously with salt, lower the heat to maintain a low boil, and add the asparagus. Cook until tender but still firm, about 3 minutes. Drain. Transfer the cooked asparagus to a large bowl of ice water to cool. Drain and set aside.

In a medium sauté pan over medium heat, add half the remaining butter. When bubbling, add the sliced mushrooms and cook, stirring, until tender, about 5 minutes. Set aside.

Pound the chicken breasts between 2 sheets of plastic wrap, one at a time, to about 1/4-inch thickness, trying not to tear them. Discard the plastic wrap and season the pounded breasts with salt and pepper. Top each breast with a slice of cheese followed by 1 red pepper half, 2 asparagus spears, and about 2 tablespoons of the mushrooms, leaving a 1/2-inch uncovered border around the pounded cutlet. Roll up cutlets tightly to enclose the stuffing, and secure the top seams, openings at both ends, and any holes, with wooden toothpicks.

Mix the flour with salt and pepper to taste in a shallow bowl, and coat the roulades evenly in the mixture. In large skillet, heat the remaining butter over medium-high heat until hot but not smoking. Add the roulades and cook until browned, about 5 minutes. Arrange the browned roulades in one layer in a small baking dish.

Deglaze the skillet with wine, scraping up any brown bits; add the brown sauce or gravy and bring to a boil. Pour a generous spoonful over each roulade and keep the remainder warm. Cover the baking dish tightly with foil and place on the middle oven rack for about 20 minutes, or until just cooked through. Using tongs, transfer the roulades to a cutting board and carefully remove wooden toothpicks. Cut each roulade in half at a 45 degree angle and place 4 halves on each plate. Spoon some of the reserved sauce over the top and serve.

Sautéed Breast of Duck with Cranberry Compote

KLAUS MULLER, CCE, AAC, DEAN, ACADEMY OF CULINARY ARTS, ATLANTIC CAPE COMMUNITY COLLEGE, MAYS LANDING, NJ

Native to North America, the cranberry was a sacred fruit and part of the folklore of American Indians. They taught early settlers to make *pemmican,* which is dried venison, buffalo, or bear preserve, pounded with lard and cranberries. This high-energy food, preserved by the benzenoic acid of the cranberry, was brought on long hunting expeditions. The acidity and tart flavor of cranberries also offers many culinary benefits—they provide a flavor contrast to sweet breads, cakes, compotes, jams, jellies, pies, and relishes. Cranberries also add a refreshing note to rich foods, such as game and nuts, cutting through the fat and complementing the taste.

MAKES 4 SERVINGS

$^1/_3$ cup red currant jelly

$^1/_4$ cup orange juice

2 tablespoons freshly squeezed lemon juice

$^1/_4$ cup port (Ruby or Tawny)

$^1/_4$ cup red wine, such as Cabernet Sauvignon
  or Merlot

$1^1/_2$ tablespoons minced fresh ginger

$^3/_4$ teaspoon Dijon mustard

$^1/_2$ teaspoon salt

Pinch cayenne pepper

Pinch ground cloves

1 cup fresh cranberries

4 boneless duck breasts (5 to 6 ounces each),
  skin on

1 tablespoon vegetable oil

Salt and freshly ground black pepper

1 teaspoon freshly grated lemon zest, optional

1 teaspoon freshly grated orange zest, optional

In a small saucepan, combine the first ten ingredients. Stir to incorporate and bring to a boil. Reduce the heat to maintain a low boil, and cook until reduced by half, about 10 minutes. Add the cranberries and cook, covered and stirring occasionally, until the cranberries are broken, 10 to 15 minutes. Remove from the heat and set aside.

Score the skin of the duck breasts, making $^1/_8$-inch-deep cuts in long diagonal lines, first in one direction and then in the opposite direction, to form a checkerboard pattern. Heat the vegetable oil in a large sauté pan, or in two medium pans, over medium-high heat. Season the duck breasts with salt and pepper, place them into the pan, and cook until browned, about 3 minutes. Turn and cook another 3 to 4 minutes for medium-rare. Transfer to a platter, loosely cover, and allow the duck breasts to rest for 5 minutes.

While the duck rests, spoon the cranberry compote in the center of each plate. Slice the duck breasts into thin diagonal slices and lay them over the compote. If desired, sprinkle the lemon and orange zest over top for a decorative touch, and serve immediately.

Cinnamon Apple Roasted Duck

RUDY GARCIA, CEC, AAC, EXECUTIVE CHEF, CULINARY ARTS,
LOS ANGELES MISSION COLLEGE, LOS ANGELES, CA

I used to know a foreign exchange student from Oaxaca, Mexico. His family raised ducks, and he told me how his mom would make duck by boiling it with cilantro, chiles, and garlic, rather like a duck stew. His family also had an apple orchard, so I created this recipe for him to bring home. *Mole* sauces are basic to Mexican cooking, and in this recipe, the *mole*-type sauce is used to baste the duck for the final ten minutes of roasting.

MAKES 4 SERVINGS

One 3- to 4-pound duck

2 tablespoons chopped fresh mint leaves

3 tablespoons minced garlic

4 tablespoons soy sauce

3 tablespoons peanut oil

2 Granny Smith apples, peeled, cored
and quartered

$^1/_2$ teaspoon ground cinnamon

2 teaspoons chopped fresh oregano,
or 1 teaspoon dried

Salt and freshly ground black pepper

FOR THE CHILE SAUCE:

12 chiles dried Anaheim chiles, seeded

$2^1/_4$ cups chicken broth

$^1/_2$ onion, diced

4 garlic cloves, minced

$^1/_4$ cup chopped flat-leaf parsley

2 tablespoons chopped cilantro

Salt and freshly ground black pepper

Preheat the oven to 350°F.

Using a sharp knife, make slits in the skin and fat on the duck breast. Trim the excess skin and fat from the neck, then run your finger under the skin, separating it from the meat. Distribute the mint and 2 tablespoons of the garlic under the skin, and pour 2 tablespoons of the soy sauce into the opening between the meat and skin. Rub the duck with the peanut oil and remaining soy sauce.

In a medium bowl, combine the apples, remaining tablespoon of garlic, and the cinnamon. Using your hands, rub the ingredients together, then place in the cavity of the duck.

Truss the duck; sprinkle with the oregano and salt and pepper. Place the duck on a roasting rack in a roasting pan and roast for 1 hour, basting with pan drippings often. The juices from the cavity should run clear and a thermometer inserted into the thickest part should read 180°F.

Meanwhile, make the chile sauce. Place the chiles into a small saucepan with 2 cups of the chicken broth, onion, and garlic. Bring to a boil, reduce the heat to low and simmer, covered, for 20 minutes. Set aside to cool slightly. Transfer the mixture to a blender, in batches if necessary, and puree until smooth, adding a little of the remaining stock, if necessary, to adjust the consistency. Return the sauce to the saucepan and bring to a boil. Remove from the heat, stir in the parsley and cilantro, and season with salt and pepper.

When the duck is done, remove it from the oven and baste it with the chile sauce. Return to the oven and roast for 10 minutes more, just long enough to form a glaze over the duck. Remove from the oven and place on a platter to rest for 10 minutes before carving.

Pilsner-Infused
Flamed Turkey Steaks

FRITZ SONNENSCHMIDT, CMC, AAC, CULINARY DEAN,
THE CULINARY INSTITUTE OF AMERICA, HYDE PARK, NY

Beer making at home has become tremendously popular in recent years. Unfortunately, not enough people cook with beer at home. Germans and Bavarians have been cooking with beer for centuries. It's great for steam-cooking fatty foods like duck, goose, and pork. In this recipe, the beer infuses the turkey with flavor.

MAKES 4 SERVINGS

4 turkey cutlets (about 6 ounces each)

6 tablespoons butter

Salt and freshly ground black pepper

2 tablespoons brandy

4 shallots, finely diced

3 tablespoons ketchup

1 teaspoon cornstarch

$^3/_4$ cup pilsner-style beer

Dash Worcestershire sauce

2 tablespoons heavy cream

1 teaspoon chopped fresh chervil,
   or $^1/_2$ teaspoon dried

Pound the turkey cutlets between 2 sheets of plastic wrap, one at a time, to about $^1/_4$-inch thickness, try not to tear them.

Heat 3 tablespoons butter in a large sauté pan over medium-high heat. When the butter has melted, season the turkey cutlets with salt and pepper and place them in one layer in the pan. Cook until lightly browned, 2 to 3 minutes, then turn and cook another 2 minutes to lightly brown the other side.

Add the brandy to the sauté pan and, with your face away from the pan, place a lit match (preferably a long match) near the brandy to ignite it. The flame will die out quickly. Transfer the cutlets to a plate. Add the remaining butter and the shallots to the pan and cook, stirring, for 1 to 2 minutes. Add the ketchup and cook, stirring, until it browns slightly. Sprinkle with the cornstarch and stir to blend. Add the beer, bring to a boil, then reduce the heat to low and simmer for 5 minutes.

Season the pan sauce with Worcestershire sauce, and salt and pepper, then return the turkey cutlets to the pan to warm. After 3 minutes, remove the turkey cutlets and place them on a servings plate. Stir the cream and chervil into the sauce, simmer for 1 to 2 minutes, then adjust the seasoning with salt and pepper. Spoon the sauce over the turkey. Serve immediately.

CHAPTER FOUR

Meat

Celebrating the Bounty of the

American Heartland and Forests

MEAT, PARTICULARLY BEEF, HAS LONG BEEN synonymous to Americans with abundance at the table. As American cuisine continues to embrace influences from around the world, we are preparing a wider variety of meats, some of which, having once enjoyed popularity with our immigrant ancestors, are at last making a long-deserved resurgence in American cooking.

Lamb is reestablishing its popularity in American cuisine after a long decline—the Herb-Roasted Leg of Lamb with White Bean, Fennel, and Olive Ragout combines traditional Italian ingredients with savory roasted lamb. And with the ready availability of farm-raised varieties, fresh game, once the mainstay of the frontier table, is garnering a new following among American cooks with dishes like the Roasted-Shallot-and-Mustard-Crusted Rabbit Loin with Chanterelles and Fava Beans.

Pork is a versatile meat that can make an elegant main course—try the Pork Loin Stuffed with Apples and Raisins, or the Bacon-Wrapped Cinnamon Pork Loin, which uses two varieties of pork, as well as fresh herbs and pine nuts. Classically-southern Smothered Pork Chops are updated here with the addition of tropical pineapple and peanut butter.

Have no fear, however—beef is not neglected here. The Sake-Glazed Stuffed Beef Tenderloin, with its Asian-inspired flavors, or the Grilled Beef Steak with Peanut-Crusted Potato Cake, which puts a nouvelle spin on the traditional meat-and-potatoes combination, are sure to satisfy the cravings of the most demanding carnivore.

Pork Loin Stuffed with Apples and Raisins

KLAUS MULLER, CCE, AAC, DEAN, ACADEMY OF CULINARY ARTS,
ATLANTIC CAPE COMMUNITY COLLEGE, MAYS LANDING, NJ

New Jersey, nicknamed the Garden State as a tribute to its rich agricultural heritage, produces a wide variety of fruits and vegetables, including apples. It is also home to many livestock farms, and wineries. This fruit-stuffed pork loin is inspired by the abundance that surrounds me.

MAKES 6 TO 8 SERVINGS

1/4 cup (1/2 stick) butter

1 cup dry white wine, such as Pinot Grigio

3 tablespoons sugar

Juice of 1 lemon

4 Granny Smith apples, peeled, cored,
   and cut into wedges

1/4 cup applejack brandy

1 cup seedless dark raisins

1/2 cup unseasoned breadcrumbs

3-pound boneless, center-cut pork loin, butterflied

Salt and freshly ground black pepper

Preheat the oven to 450°F.

In a large sauté pan, heat the butter over medium-high heat. When it has melted, add the white wine, sugar, and lemon juice, and bring to a boil. Cook until the liquid is reduced by half, then add the apples and applejack. Cook, gently stirring occasionally, until the apples are tender but still firm, 5 to 7 minutes, depending on the thickness of the wedges. Add the raisins and breadcrumbs, and stir. Transfer the mixture to a bowl. Set aside to cool slightly.

Generously season the pork loin with salt and pepper. Lay the pork flat on a clean work surface and spread the apple/raisin mixture evenly down the center, stopping 1 1/2 to 2 inches before reaching the ends. Fold the sides of the meat over the filling to make a tight roll, securely tying with kitchen string.

Transfer the stuffed pork roll to a medium roasting pan and place on the middle rack of the oven. After 15 minutes, reduce the oven temperature to 350°F. Roast for 1 more hour, then check the temperature with a meat thermometer. It is cooked when the thermometer registers 150°F; it might require another 15 minutes. Remove the pan from the oven and transfer the pork to a plate to rest for 10 minutes before slicing.

Bacon-Wrapped Cinnamon Pork Loin

RUDY GARCIA, CEC, AAC, EXECUTIVE CHEF, CULINARY ARTS,
LOS ANGELES MISSION COLLEGE, LOS ANGELES, CA

As recently as seventy-five years ago, California's San Fernando Valley, including the areas now known as Burbank and Glendale, was nothing but farmland. Many of the farmers raised pork in this 50-square-mile region, about 25 miles from downtown Los Angeles. The technique of wrapping the pork in bacon adds a smoky flavor to the pork. More importantly, the bacon keeps the pork moist when cooking—the lean pork loin would dry out otherwise. Pine nuts are often used in *mole* sauces, along with other nuts like peanuts, almonds, walnuts, or pumpkin seeds.

MAKES 10 SERVINGS

2 tablespoons peanut oil

1/2 cup pine nuts (pignoli)

1 tablespoon minced garlic

1/2 onion, diced

2 tablespoons chopped cilantro

2 tablespoons chopped fresh mint

1 tablespoon sesame oil

2 teaspoons ground cinnamon

3 pounds boneless center-cut pork loin, butterflied

Salt and ground white pepper

6 slices uncooked slab bacon

Preheat the oven to 350°F.

Heat the peanut oil in a small skillet over medium heat. When hot, add the pine nuts and garlic and cook, stirring, until lightly browned, 3 to 4 minutes. Transfer to a medium bowl to cool.

Add the onion, cilantro, mint, sesame oil, and cinnamon to the bowl and stir to blend. Rub this mixture all over the pork loin. Roll the pork loin into a cylinder, tying in places to keep it closed and uniform. Season with salt and white pepper; wrap the bacon slices around the meat. Place the pork on a roasting rack set in a medium roasting pan. Roast for 50 minutes or until a meat thermometer inserted in the center registers 150°F. Transfer the pork to a warm platter and set aside to rest for 10 minutes. Note that the meat will continue to cook while it rests. Slice the pork into 1/4-inch slices and serve.

Pistachio-Crusted Pork Scaloppine with Mango Shrimp

HEINZ SOWINSKI, CEC, AAC, OWNER, LA MAISON ON TELFAIR, AUGUSTA, GA

Sweet, pink shrimp from the Florida Keys inspired this dish. To create an island feel, I added the flavors of peppers, mangos, and tender pork. It is one of the most requested dishes in my restaurant, where I like serving it with Basmati rice and fresh, steamed asparagus.

MAKES 4 SERVINGS

1 tablespoon olive oil

$1/2$ red bell pepper, julienned

$1/2$ yellow bell pepper, julienned

2 tablespoons capers

$1/2$ cup prepared sweet-and-sour or margarita mix (available in beverage stores and in many supermarkets)

$3/4$ cup heavy cream

$1/2$ cup thinly sliced fresh mango

1 teaspoon Tabasco sauce

Salt and freshly ground black pepper

Four 3-ounce pieces of pork loin or eight $1^1/2$-ounce pieces of tenderloin

$1/2$ cup all-purpose flour

1 teaspoon salt

$2/3$ cup chopped pistachio nuts

$1/3$ cup unseasoned fresh breadcrumbs

1 large egg

2 tablespoons water

6 tablespoons peanut oil (as needed)

6 medium shrimp, peeled and deveined, cut in half crosswise

Preheat the oven to 250°F.

In a medium, nonstick sauté pan, heat the olive oil over medium-high heat. Add the peppers and capers and cook, stirring, 2 minutes. Add the sweet-and-sour or margarita mix, bring to a boil, and cook until slightly thickened and reduced by half, 3 to 5 minutes. Stir in the cream, mango, and Tabasco. Simmer another 3 minutes, or until the sauce is thick enough to coat the back of a spoon. Season with salt and pepper to taste. Cover and set aside.

Place each piece of pork between 2 sheets of plastic wrap and pound them until they are slightly less than $1/4$ inch thick. Set aside.

Combine the flour with the teaspoon of salt and spread onto a large plate. Mix the pistachios and the breadcrumbs on a separate plate. Lightly beat the egg with the water in a shallow bowl or a dish with sides.

Heat 4 tablespoons of the peanut oil in a large skillet over medium-high heat. When the oil is very hot, dredge the pork cutlets in the flour, dip them in the egg, then lay them in the pistachio nuts, sprinkling any bare spots to cover. Add them to the skillet as they're ready, but do not crowd the pan. Cook in batches, if necessary, adding more oil as needed. Turn the cutlets as they brown, taking care not to burn the nuts, and cook the other side, 2 to $2^1/2$ minutes per side. Transfer the cooked pork to an ovenproof platter and place in the oven to keep warm.

Add the shrimp to the hot skillet and cook for 15 to 30 seconds per side. Arrange 3 shrimp on top of each portion of pork and spoon some of the mango sauce over top.

Roasted Pork Tenderloin in Sausage Crust with Beet Mashed Potatoes

RUDY GARCIA, CEC, AAC, EXECUTIVE CHEF, CULINARY ARTS, LOS ANGELES MISSION COLLEGE, LOS ANGELES, CA

I created this central-Mexico style recipe at a gastronomic festival that's held in Puerto Viarta every November. Don't be put off by quantity of chiles in this recipe—the dried ancho chile, commonly used in Mexican *mole* sauces, is very mild, with a striking deep-red color. The mashed potatoes will be dark lavender in color when mashed with the beets. You can substitute golden beets, and though the flavor will be just as good, the presentation won't be as dramatic.

MAKES 6 TO 8 SERVINGS

Preheat the oven to 375°F.

FOR THE SAUSAGE CRUST:

1 small onion, diced

1 cup chicken stock

1 pound ground pork

1 teaspoon poultry seasoning

1 teaspoon caraway seeds

2 tablespoons chopped fresh parsley

1 tablespoon chopped fresh basil

4 tablespoons peanut oil

3 pork tenderloins (about 1 pound each)

Salt and freshly ground black pepper

TO PREPARE THE SAUSAGE CRUST:

Combine all of the ingredients in a medium bowl.

Heat 2 tablespoons of the peanut oil in a large ovenproof skillet over medium-high heat. Season the pork tenderloins with salt and pepper. When the oil is almost smoking, place the tenderloins into the skillet. Do not crowd; if your pan isn't large enough, cook in two batches. Cook until browned all over, about 8 minutes. Transfer to a large plate. Set aside to cool. Wipe the skillet, add the remaining 2 tablespoons oil, and place it over medium heat.

Pat the crust mixture evenly on the tenderloins. Place them in the skillet and sear, turning to brown all over, 5 to 7 minutes. Transfer the skillet into the oven and cook another 10 minutes, or until the internal temperature is 145°F. Let the meat rest before slicing into thick slices. The meat will continue to cook as it rests.

1 pound dried ancho chiles

1 cup chopped onion

¼ cup minced garlic

1 quart chicken stock

Salt and freshly ground black pepper

Grilled pineapple rings for garnish, optional

4 pounds potatoes

1 pound beets

½ cup roasted garlic (see Note)

½ pound (2 sticks) butter, softened

Salt and freshly ground black pepper

Separate, but do not peel the cloves from 2 to 3 heads of garlic. Lightly brush the cloves with vegetable oil and roast for 10 to 15 minutes at 350°F. When cool, pinch the cloves. The meat will slip right out.

Remove the stems from the chiles and add to a large pot with the onion, garlic, and chicken stock. Bring to a boil, then reduce the heat, and simmer for 15 minutes. Remove the garlic, onion and chiles from the liquid; reserve solids and liquid. Transfer the garlic, onion, and chiles to a food processor or blender and puree. Add about 2 cups of the reserved liquid and process again. Add additional stock, if necessary, to create a thick sauce.

Boil the potatoes and beets in a large pot of boiling water until tender, 20 to 30 minutes. Remove from the pot, drain, and let cool. Remove the skins from the potatoes and beets, and transfer to a mixing bowl. With a mixer, beat the potatoes and beets with the roasted garlic and butter until well mashed. Add salt and pepper to taste.

To serve, put a mound of the mashed potatoes on each plate. Cut each pork tenderloin on the bias into two pieces like a spear. Transfer the pork to the serving plates, along with the grilled pineapple, if using. Dollop the ancho chile sauce around the edge of plate.

Smothered Pork Chops

GEORGE J. PASTOR, ED.D, CEC, CCE, AAC,
HILLSBOROUGH COMMUNITY COLLEGE, TAMPA, FL

Here's a new recipe for a favorite, classic southern dish. Pork is commonly paired with apples, apricots, and other fruits, but I thought that pineapple would give this dish some tropical flair.

MAKES 4 SERVINGS

Four ½-inch-thick boneless pork chops
   (about 5 ounces each)

Salt and freshly ground black pepper

2 tablespoons vegetable oil

½ cup apple cider vinegar

One 5½ ounce can crushed pineapple in juice

½ cup crunchy peanut butter

1 tablespoon granulated sugar

½ cup water, as needed

Sprinkle the chops with salt and pepper. In a large sauté pan with a lid, heat the oil over medium-high heat. When almost smoking, place the chops into the pan, raise the heat to high, and carefully tilt and shake the pan to evenly distribute the oil. Brown the chops on both sides, about 2 minutes per side, then transfer to a large plate.

Lower the heat to medium-low and pour the cider vinegar into the pan. Using a wooden spoon, stir, scrapping the bottom of the pan to release the flavorful bits stuck to the bottom. Add the pineapple and its juice, peanut butter, and sugar, stirring until completely incorporated. Return the pork chops to the pan, reduce the heat to low, and cover. Cook for 15 minutes, turning the chops once or twice, and adding the water as necessary to keep cooking sauce moist, until the chops are tender. Serve smothered with the cooking sauce.

Beef Stroganoff

JOHN CARROLL, CEC, AAC, DIXVILLE NOTCH, NH

Named after the nineteenth-century Russian diplomat Count Paul Stroganov, this traditional dish became the rage in America during the nineteen-fifties. In my native Vermont, I have served this dish many times because it is a simple and elegant meal that can easily be prepared in advance, allowing me to enjoy my guests. This hearty dish is perfect with buttered noodles, particularly when there's a chill in the air.

MAKES 4 SERVINGS

¼ cup (½ stick) butter

1 onion, chopped

1 garlic clove, minced

¼ cup all-purpose flour

1 cup beef broth

1 cup pitted black olives, sliced

½ cup tomato paste

3 tablespoons olive oil

1½ pounds beef tenderloin,
    cut into ½-inch-thick strips

Salt and freshly ground black pepper

½ pound white mushrooms, brushed clean,
    trimmed, and sliced

¼ cup brandy

2 teaspoons chopped fresh dill

1 cup sour cream

In a large sauté pan, heat the butter over medium heat. When bubbly, add the onion and garlic and cook, stirring, until soft, about 5 minutes. Reduce the heat to medium-low, sprinkle the flour into the pan and cook, stirring to incorporate and prevent sticking, about 5 minutes. Whisk in the beef broth and bring to a boil. Lower the heat to a simmer. Stir in the olives and the tomato paste.

In a separate large sauté pan or skillet, heat 1½ tablespoons of the olive oil over medium-high heat, 3 to 4 minutes, or until almost smoking. Season the beef strips with salt and pepper and add to the pan. Cook, stirring occasionally, until evenly browned. Transfer the beef to the pan with the simmering beef broth. Add the remaining 1½ tablespoons oil to the hot pan used to cook the beef, add the mushrooms and cook, stirring, until they are lightly browned, 3 to 5 minutes. Remove the pan from the heat, add the brandy, and stir, scraping the bottom of the pan to loosen any browned bits. Transfer the mushrooms and their liquid to the sauté pan with the beef. Cook, simmering, stirring occasionally, 15 minutes. Add the sour cream and dill and cook another 10 minutes. Adjust the seasonings and serve.

Sake-Glazed Stuffed Beef Tenderloin

STAFFORD T. DE CAMBRA, CEC, CCE, AAC, SENIOR EXECUTIVE CHEF,
S.S. INDEPENDENCE, AMERICAN HAWAII CRUISES

East meets West in almost every aspect of Hawaiian life. This is particularly true of the cuisine. This recipe reflects one of the hottest trends in cooking today—the flavors of the Pacific Rim. I prefer to use local ingredients like Hawaiian raw cane sugar and macadamia nut oil, but you can get good results with the suggested substitutions.

MAKES 4 SERVINGS

1¹/₂ cups *mirin* (sweet rice wine)

1¹/₂ cups low-sodium soy sauce

1 cup premium Japanese *sake*

³/₄ cup Hawaiian raw cane sugar or
dark brown sugar

8 ounces shiitake mushrooms, stems removed,
caps julienned

4 large egg whites

1 bunch fresh basil, stems removed and discarded,
leaves cut into thin ribbons

3 ounces dried papaya, cut into strips

1¹/₂ to 2 pounds beef tenderloin

¹/₄ cup macadamia nut oil or peanut oil

Preheat the oven to 350°F.

To prepare the sake glaze, place the *mirin*, soy sauce, *sake*, and sugar in a medium saucepan and stir to combine. Bring to a boil, then adjust the heat to maintain a slow boil. Cook, stirring occasionally, until reduced by half. Set aside, cover to keep warm.

In a medium bowl, combine the mushrooms, egg whites, basil, and papaya, and mix well.

Cut a long incision down the length of the beef tenderloin, butterflying it, then lay it out flat. Spread the mushroom stuffing mixture evenly over the meat, leaving a 1-inch border on all sides. Roll the tenderloin up and tie it with string.

Heat the oil in a large, ovenproof sauté pan over medium-high heat. When almost smoking, lay the tenderloin in the pan and cook, turning to brown evenly on all sides.

Transfer the pan to the oven and cook, basting frequently with the sake glaze, for 15 minutes. When the thermometer registers 125° to 130°F on meat thermometer, it is medium-rare. (Note that the temperature of the meat will rise another five degrees while it sits after cooking.) If you prefer your meat done further, you can cook it to 135° to 140°F. Set aside to rest for 5 minutes before carving into ¹/₂-inch-thick slices.

Roulade of Beef

KLAUS MULLER, CCE, AAC, DEAN, ACADEMY OF CULINARY ARTS,
ATLANTIC CAPE COMMUNITY COLLEGE, MAYS LANDING, NJ

The roulade, or rolled meat or fish with a filling, is a concept that exists in many countries. This version, rolled beef wrapped in bacon, most resembles a German dish; the Italian *braciole* is made from pounded beef, rolled with a filling of cheese and herbs; and *paupiette* is a French version, usually made from fish, using flounder or salmon fillets. These days, Americans often make roulades from pounded chicken and turkey breasts. It's a technique that allows you to be creative, have fun in the kitchen, and use whatever ingredients that look best at the market.

MAKES 4 SERVINGS

8 thin slices bottom or top round
   (3 to 3¹/₄ ounces each)

Salt and freshly ground black pepper

2 tablespoons prepared mustard

4 bacon strips, halved

1 small onion, cut into 8 wedges

¹/₂ dill pickle, cut into 8 slices

2 tablespoons vegetable oil

1 small carrot, peeled and diced

1 celery stalk, diced

¹/₂ small onion, diced

3 tablespoons tomato paste

¹/₄ cup dry red wine

2 whole cloves

1 bay leaf

1 small clove garlic, minced

¹/₄ teaspoon white peppercorns, crushed

¹/₈ teaspoon dried thyme

¹/₄ cup all-purpose flour

3 cups beef stock or water

Preheat the oven to 350°F.

Place the meat slices on a clean flat surface and season with salt and pepper. Spread the mustard over the top of each slice, then place a slice of bacon, 1 wedge of onion, and 1 piece of dill pickle over the mustard. Roll the meat, lengthwise, forming roulades, and secure closed with toothpicks.

Heat the oil in a large sauté pan over medium-high heat. Add the roulades and brown on all sides. Transfer the roulades to a plate and add the carrot, celery, and diced onion to the pan. Cook, stirring, until lightly browned, about 3 minutes. Stir in the tomato paste, and cook until it begins to brown, another minute. Add the red wine, cloves, bay leaf, garlic, peppercorns, and thyme, and stir to loosen any flavorful bits adhered to the bottom of the pan. Stir in the flour, cook for 1 minute, and add the stock or water. Bring to a boil, return the roulades to the pan, cover and transfer to the preheated oven. Cook until the meat is very tender, no more than 30 minutes.

Remove the roulades from the sauce and discard the toothpicks. Remove any fat from the surface of the sauce; adjust the seasoning with salt and pepper. Strain the sauce. Serve the roulades with sauce spooned over top.

Braised Chuck Eye Chop with Lemon

EDWARD G. LEONARD, CMC, AAC,
FOOD 1ST RESTAURANT CORP., NORWALK, CT

This recipe turns tough but very flavorful chuck eye cuts into fork-tender steaks. Serve the braised chops and their sauce over tagliatelle or noodles that have been tossed with Parmesan cheese and extra-virgin olive oil.

MAKES 6 SERVINGS

3 lemons

3 tablespoons unsalted butter

3 tablespoons olive oil

1 cup all-purpose flour

6 chuck eye chops

Salt and freshly ground black pepper

Pinch dry sage

2 shallots, diced

3 cloves garlic, thinly sliced

¼ cup diced fennel bulb

¼ cup diced carrots

2 cups sliced white button or crimini mushrooms

¼ cup dry white wine

3 plum tomatoes, diced

10 ounces chicken stock

10 ounces demi-glace (available in specialty food markets)

3 tablespoons chopped flat-leaf parsley

Preheat the oven to 325°F.

Using a sharp knife, peel the lemons, removing all the skin and the underlying bitter white pith. The flesh of the fruit should be totally exposed. Over a bowl, cut between the membranes on the sides of each segment to release them. Set aside.

In a large sauté pan over medium-high heat, heat 1 tablespoon of the butter and the olive oil. Spread the flour on a plate. Season the chops with salt and pepper and sage, and dredge them in the flour, shaking off any excess. Lay the chops into the sauté pan and cook until nicely browned on both sides, about 5 minutes. Transfer the chops to a platter.

If necessary, add another tablespoon of butter to the sauté pan. Add the shallots, garlic, fennel, and carrots. Cook, stirring, until lightly browned, 2 to 3 minutes. Add the sliced mushrooms and cook, stirring, for 6 to 8 minutes. Deglaze the pan with the wine, stirring with a wooden spoon to loosen any browned bits on the bottom of the pan. Add the tomatoes, stock, and demi-glace. Bring to a boil, cover, and transfer to the preheated oven. Cook for 50 minutes; turn the chops and cook another 30 minutes, or until very tender.

Using kitchen tongs or a slotted spoon, place a chop on each plate. Stir the lemon segments into the pan juices, stir in the remaining butter, and spoon the sauce over the chops. Sprinkle with the parsley and serve.

Braised Short Ribs

THOMAS A. BERG, CEC, AAC, CHEF/OWNER,
THOMAS BERG CATERING, MINNEAPOLIS, MN

I love to make this traditional Jewish meal on a cold day—not an uncommon occurrence in Minnesota—letting it braise and perfume the air for much of the day. If time permits, and you can resist digging in immediately, cover, refrigerate, and skim off the surface fat the next day. Serve with oven-roasted potatoes and carrots.

MAKES 6 SERVINGS

5 tablespoons vegetable oil

1 cup all-purpose flour, for dredging

6 beef short ribs, 4 to 5 inches each (about 5 pounds total)

Salt and freshly ground black pepper

1/2 cup beef stock

1 cup tomato sauce

2 large onions, chopped

1 tablespoon minced garlic

1/3 cup dark brown sugar

Preheat the oven to 350°F.

Heat 3 tablespoons of the oil in a large, heavy skillet over medium-high heat.

Place the flour on a large, shallow bowl or plate. Sprinkle the short ribs all over with salt and pepper. Dredge 3 ribs in the flour, turn to coat, shake off the excess, and place them into the hot oil. Cook until well-browned, about 4 minutes, then turn to brown the other side. Transfer to a large bowl. Heat the remaining oil, and repeat with the remaining 3 ribs. Add these to the bowl and set aside.

In a sauté or braising pan large enough to hold all the ribs in one layer (at least 12 inches), stir together the beef stock, tomato sauce, onions, garlic, and brown sugar. Place over medium-high heat and bring to a boil. Reduce the heat, and simmer, stirring often, 15 to 20 minutes. Place the browned ribs in the pan in one layer. Cover tightly and bake for 3 hours, until the meat is very tender.

Richville Roast Veal

JOHN ZEHNDER, CEC, AAC, EXECUTIVE CHEF,
ZEHNDER'S RESTAURANT, FRANKENMUTH, MI

About twenty years ago, a local lumberyard owner asked me to serve a traditional dish, which he called Richville Veal, at a special party that he was going to host. Richville is a small Michigan village with a history dating back more than 175 years. Unfamiliar with the dish, I asked him to provide a recipe. I received six aged, handwritten pages containing different versions of the recipe, each with slight variations in the ingredients. With the help of my staff we prepared each one. After tasting them, I incorporated the best elements of each into one terrific recipe. This heirloom dish is best served with homemade noodles or spaetzle.

MAKES 6 SERVINGS

2 pounds veal leg roast, boned

1 cup all-purpose flour

1 cup vegetable oil

1 medium onion, sliced

1 cup veal or chicken stock

2 teaspoons salt

1 teaspoon cracked black pepper

1 teaspoon garlic salt

3 bay leaves

$^1/_2$ cup water

Preheat the oven to 350°F.

Cut the veal into 4-inch x 4-inch x 2-inch chunks. Remove all the tendons and silver.

Spread $^3/_4$ cup of the flour on a plate. Add the vegetable oil to a large sauté pan or casserole to a depth of $^1/_2$ inch; set over medium-high heat. Coat the veal pieces lightly with the flour, shake off the excess, and add to the pan. Cook, in two batches if necessary, to prevent crowding. Turn to brown well on all sides. Transfer the veal to a platter.

There should still be fat in the pan. Set the pan over medium heat, and add the onion. Cook, stirring, until softened, about 5 minutes. Add the stock to the pan. Using a wooden spoon, stir, scraping the bottom of the pan to loosen any browned bits. Season with salt and pepper to taste. Add the garlic salt and bay leaves. Bring to a boil, then reduce heat to keep at a simmer.

In a small bowl, stir the remaining flour into the water. When smooth, add to the pan, stirring to blend. Return the veal to the pan, cover, and transfer to the preheated oven. If your pan doesn't have a lid, cover it tightly with aluminum foil. Cook for 2 hours, or until the veal is very tender.

Grilled Beef Steak with Peanut-Crusted Potato Cake

BOB BURNS, CEC, AAC, EXECUTIVE CHEF,
COLUMBUS COUNTRY CLUB, COLUMBUS, OH

This recipe, which won the 1998 Ohio Best of Beef Chefs Challenge, is a reinterpretation of the classic American meal—meat and potatoes. The vibrant steak marinade combines such Mexican ingredients as jalapeño peppers and cilantro with popular Asian ingredients like curry powder and coconut milk. Pair that with the potato cakes, crispy on the outside and soft on the inside, and you've created something altogether new.

MAKES 8 SERVINGS

FOR THE POTATO CAKES:

10 ounces Idaho potatoes
    (about 2 medium), peeled

1 large egg

1 cup water

1/2 cup all-purpose flour

Salt and freshly ground black pepper

1/2 cup chopped peanuts

2 to 3 cups peanut oil for frying

4 tablespoons butter

1/4 cup minced onion

2 cloves garlic, minced

2 teaspoons brown sugar

1/3 cup heavy cream

2 large egg yolks

FOR THE STEAK:

1/2 jalapeño pepper, seeded and minced

1 cup chopped cilantro

6 cloves garlic, chopped

7 tablespoons olive oil

4 teaspoons dark brown sugar

2 1/2 teaspoons curry powder

3/4 teaspoon turmeric

3/4 teaspoon salt

1/2 teaspoon freshly ground black pepper

1 cup coconut milk

8 New York strip steaks (6 to 8 ounces each)

TO PREPARE THE STEAK:

Combine all the ingredients, except for the steaks, in a medium bowl, and stir to blend. Place the steaks in one layer in a baking dish and pour the marinade over them. Cover and refrigerate, at least 2 hours.

MEANWHILE, PREPARE THE POTATO CAKES:

Place the potatoes in a medium saucepan, cover with water and bring to a boil. Lower the heat to maintain a slow boil. Cook until a sharp knife can easily pierce the flesh, about 20 minutes. Drain. Put the potatoes through a food mill (ricer). Transfer to a large bowl. (recipe continues on p.106)

Grilled Beef Steak with
Peanut-Crusted Potato Cake (continued)

Preheat the oven to 250°F. Preheat the grill. In a large sauté pan or Dutch oven, heat the peanut oil over medium-high heat.

In a medium bowl, beat the egg with water. In another medium bowl, generously season the flour with salt and pepper. Spread the peanuts out on a plate.

In a large skillet, heat butter over medium-high heat. Add the onions and garlic and cook, stirring, about 5 minutes. Stir in the brown sugar. Cook, stirring, 5 to 7 minutes, until well caramelized. Transfer to the bowl with the potatoes. Beat in the heavy cream and the egg yolks. When thoroughly combined, form 8 potato patties.

Place the patties, one by one, into the flour, turning to evenly coat. Dip each potato patty in the egg mixture, then coat with the chopped peanuts. Place the patties, a few at a time, in the hot oil and cook, turning once, until golden brown, about 2 minutes per side. As they're finished, blot dry with a paper towel and transfer to a plate. Place the plate in the preheated oven to keep warm.

Grill the steaks, about 3 minutes per side for medium-rare. Let the steaks rest for 5 minutes, then slice into ¹/₂-inch-thick slices on the bias. Serve with the fried potato cakes.

Stuffed Cabbage Rolls

THOMAS A. BERG, CEC, AAC, CHEF/OWNER,
THOMAS BERG CATERING, MINNEAPOLIS, MN

As a cold-weather crop, cabbage thrives in Minnesota and is appreciated by the many Scandinavians and Middle Europeans who settled here. Almost every culture in Central Europe has its own version of stuffed cabbage. In this recipe, the savory meat and slight acidity from the tomato sauce contrast nicely with the sweet fruit.

MAKES 6 SERVINGS

3 tablespoons margarine

1½ cups chopped onions

½ cup dark brown sugar

One 35-ounce can peeled tomatoes in juice

2 cups tomato sauce

Juice of 1 lemon

1 head green cabbage (about 3 pounds)

2 pounds ground beef or ground turkey

1 small onion, grated

3 eggs, lightly beaten

¼ cup white rice

2 tablespoons ketchup

Salt and freshly ground black pepper

8 ounces pitted prunes, chopped

½ cup dark raisins

Juice of 1 lemon

Fill large pot (big enough to hold the cabbage) ⅔ full of water. Bring to a boil and salt.

To prepare the sauce, heat the margarine in a medium saucepan set over medium heat until melted. Add the chopped onions and cook, stirring, until soft and lightly browned, about 10 minutes. Add the brown sugar and tomatoes, crushing them with your fingers as you add them to the pan (with their juice), and tomato sauce and lemon juice. Stir, bring to a boil, then reduce heat to low and cover. Cook, stirring occasionally, for 1½ hours.

Preheat the oven to 350°F. Lightly grease a large, nonreactive baking dish and set aside.

While the sauce cooks, prepare the cabbage. Using a paring knife, cut a cone-shaped incision in the bottom of the cabbage to remove the core. Place the cored cabbage into the boiling water, reduce the heat, and simmer, 15 minutes. Drain, cover with cold water and drain again. When cool enough to handle, peel off the leaves, trying not to tear them. Trim thick ribs from the leaves. You should have 16 to 20 relatively intact leaves. Set aside.

To prepare the filling, combine the ground beef with the grated onion, eggs, rice, and ketchup; season with salt and pepper. Mix by hand, adding up to ½ cup of water if necessary, until mixture is moist but still thick.

Place about ¼ cup of the meat filling in the center of each leaf. Fold the bottom of the leaf over the filling, fold in the sides, then roll to enclose securely. Repeat with the remaining filling and cabbage leaves. Arrange the packages, seam side down, on the prepared baking dish. Sprinkle with the prunes and raisins and spoon the tomato sauce over top. Cover the baking dish and bake for 1½ hours.

Roasted-Shallot-and-Mustard-Crusted Rabbit Loin with Chanterelles and Fava Beans

VINCENT ALBERICI, AAC, EXECUTIVE CHEF,
ADAM'S MARK HOTEL, PHILADELPHIA, PA

I use a local breed of rabbit raised in central Pennsylvania, but you will find the loin of any young rabbit to be tender, juicy, and mild. This savory golden crust is a perfect match for the earthy chanterelle mushrooms and buttery, nutty fava beans.

MAKES 6 TO 8 SERVINGS

2 tablespoons mustard seeds

10 shallots (about 6 ounces), peeled

Cloves from 2 heads of garlic, peeled

1 cup olive oil

2 tablespoons red-wine vinegar

1 tablespoon fresh chopped thyme (leaves only), or $\frac{1}{2}$ teaspoon dried

1 chopped sorrel leaf, or 8 chopped spinach leaves

2 boneless rabbit loins (1 pound each)

Salt and freshly ground black pepper

$\frac{1}{2}$ cup unseasoned fresh bread crumbs

2 tablespoons minced shallots

2 teaspoons minced garlic

8 ounces chanterelle mushrooms, brushed clean

$\frac{1}{2}$ cup diced tomato

2 cups fresh shelled fava beans

2 cups chicken stock

2 teaspoons fresh chopped sage

Preheat the oven to 350°F.

Place the mustard seeds in a small skillet and set over medium heat, stirring, until lightly browned, about 5 minutes. Set aside.

In a small baking pan, combine the shallots, garlic, and olive oil. Place the pan in the oven and roast, 30 minutes, or until the shallots and garlic are very tender. Drain, reserving $\frac{1}{2}$ cup oil for later use. Do not turn off the oven.

Place the roasted shallots and garlic, mustard seeds, vinegar, thyme, and sorrel leaf in the work bowl of a food processor and process until creamy. Set aside.

Season the rabbit loins with salt and pepper. Heat $\frac{1}{4}$ cup of the reserved shallot-garlic oil in a large sauté pan over medium-high heat. When hot, place the rabbit loins into the pan and brown on all sides. The total cooking time will be about 6 minutes. Transfer to a plate and set aside to cool.

Spread the breadcrumbs in an even layer on a large plate. Rub the shallot and garlic puree over the rabbit loins, then roll them in the breadcrumbs to evenly coat. Place in a roasting pan and roast for 6 to 8 minutes.

Meanwhile, prepare the chanterelles and fava beans. In a medium saucepan, heat the remaining $1/4$ cup of shallot-garlic oil over medium-high heat. Add the pureed shallots and garlic and cook, stirring, 1 minute. Add the chanterelles and cook, gently stirring, until golden, about 5 minutes. Add the tomatoes, cook another minute, then add the fava beans and stock. Simmer, 2 to 3 minutes, then remove the pan from the heat and season with sage, salt and pepper, stirring to combine.

Slice each cooked rabbit loin into about 6 slices. Transfer some of the fava bean mixture to the center of each serving plate, fan the rabbit slices over the top, and serve.

Herb-Roasted Leg of Lamb with White Bean, Fennel & Olive Ragout

VINCENT ALBERICI, AAC, EXECUTIVE CHEF,
ADAM'S MARK HOTEL, PHILADELPHIA, PA

Lamb is a popular ingredient throughout Italy. In the past, however, most Italians' diets consisted mainly of peasant foods like polenta and risotto (both of which have become quite chic in recent years), and meat was an accompaniment. Italian immigrants to America found that meat was both abundant and affordable; and the tradition of the Sunday feast was born.

MAKES 8 SERVINGS

FOR THE LAMB:

Grated zest of 2 lemons

3 bay leaves

1 tablespoon chopped fresh rosemary,
  or 1 teaspoon dried

1 tablespoon chopped fresh oregano,
  or 1 teaspoon dried

6 cloves garlic, minced

1 tablespoon kosher salt

2 teaspoons cracked black peppercorns

1 teaspoon crushed red pepper flakes

One 5- to 6-pound deboned leg of lamb

2 cups plus 3 tablespoons vegetable oil

1 cup Chardonnay wine

2 tablespoons unsalted butter

8 sprigs fresh mint, chopped

TO PREPARE THE LEG OF LAMB:

In a small bowl, combine the lemon zest, bay leaves, rosemary, oregano, garlic, salt, black peppercorns, and red pepper. Rub this mixture evenly over the leg of lamb. Place in a deep stainless steel pan and coat with the 2 cups of oil. Refrigerate, to marinate, for 24 hours.

Preheat the oven to 350°F.

Remove the lamb from the oil, drain, and pat dry with paper towels. Heat the 3 tablespoons of oil in a large sauté pan over medium-high heat. When the oil is very hot, add the lamb, and sear for 1 to 2 minutes on each side. Once browned, transfer to a roasting rack.

Put the rack in a roasting pan and transfer to the preheated oven. Cook for about 1½ hours, turning once, until the internal temperature reaches 140°F on a meat thermometer (medium rare). Note that the meat temperature will rise about 5 additional degrees upon sitting. Transfer the lamb to a serving platter and let rest for at least 15 minutes before slicing. (recipe continues on following page)

Herb-Roasted Leg of Lamb with
White Bean, Fennel & Olive Ragout (continued)

(continued)

FOR THE RAGOUT:

2 tablespoons olive oil

1 small fennel bulb, thinly sliced

1 tablespoon minced shallots

1 teaspoon minced garlic

2 plum tomatoes, diced

1 cup cooked or canned, drained white beans

1 cooked artichoke (see Note), cut into quarters

$1/4$ teaspoon saffron

$1/2$ cup Chardonnay wine

1 cup chicken stock

Juice of 2 lemons

Zest of 1 lemon

$1/3$ cup pitted niçoise olives

1 teaspoon chopped fresh oregano,
     or $1/4$ teaspoon dried

1 teaspoon chopped fresh thyme,
     or $1/4$ teaspoon dried

2 tablespoons extra-virgin olive oil

Salt and freshly ground pepper

While the lamb cooks, prepare the white bean, fennel, and olive ragout. Heat the oil in a medium sauté pan set over medium heat. Add the fennel and cook, stirring, until tender, about 5 minutes. Stir in the shallots and garlic, cook 30 seconds. Add the tomato and cook another minute. Add the white beans, artichoke, and saffron and cook, stirring, until hot. Add the wine. Allow the wine to reduce by half, then add the stock, lemon juice, and lemon zest. Simmer for 2 minutes. Remove from the heat and stir in the olives, herbs, and olive oil. Season to taste with salt and pepper. Set aside, covered, to keep warm.

Skim the fat from the roasting pan, then place over medium-high heat on top of the stove. Add the Chardonnay to the pan to deglaze, scraping to loosen the caramelized bits from the pan. Simmer until reduced to a rich, natural glaze, about 3 minutes. Remove from the heat. Add the butter and mint to the pan. Add salt and pepper to taste.

Serve this meal family style, with the sliced lamb on one platter and the white bean ragout in a bowl.

TO COOK THE ARTICHOKE

Using a large knife, trim the pointed top from the artichoke. Then, using scissors, cut the thorny tips from the remaining leaves. Leave the stem attached, but peel the tough outer layer with a sharp knife or peeler. Boil the artichoke in $1^{1}/_{2}$ quarts of water in a medium saucepan, with a small lid or heat-resistant plate on top of the artichoke to keep it submerged. Cook for 35 minutes or until a leaf can easily be pulled from the base. Drain and let cool. When cool enough to handle, squeeze any excess water from the artichoke and cut in half lengthwise. Cut each half again, so that you have quarters. Remove and discard the fuzzy choke from the center.

CARVING A LEG OF LAMB

Once the lamb is properly roasted, allow it to rest before carving. Remember to reserve the bone, which can be used to flavor soup. This same basic procedure could be followed for other leg cuts (ham or venison, for example). The method for carving a leg of lamb is as follows:

1. Steady the leg by holding the shank end with a clean kitchen towel. Begin by cutting away the end piece (Fig. 1).

2. The initial cuts are made vertically, until the bone is reached (Fig. 2).

3. Angle the knife slightly as you continue cutting, so that the cuts remain similar in size (Fig. 3).

4. When the slices become very large, begin alternating the cutting angle, first from the left side, then from the right (Fig. 4). This will further help to insure consistently sized slices.

1.

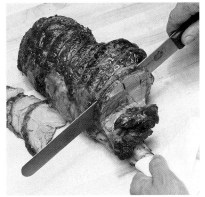

2.

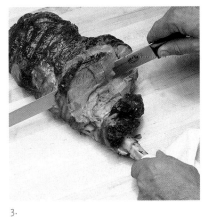

3.

4.

CHAPTER FIVE

Seafood

*Fresh Fish and Shellfish from
the Oceans, Lakes, and Rivers*

AMERICA'S COASTAL WATERS AND INLAND LAKES
are renowned for their abundance and variety. From
Maine to California, our waters are alive with un-
usual and delicious species, and modern distribution methods
allow us to enjoy the availability of a wide variety of fresh
seafood year-round.

Trout fishing is a great American pastime. The Brook Trout
with Hazelnut Crust and Warm Asparagus Salad is inspired by the
ingredients available near Colorado's Snake River, while the
Whole Trout with Herbs and Foamy Butter Sauce is a tribute to
the resurgent bounty of the Hudson River. Bluefish, another popular American sport fish known as the "bulldog of the ocean" for its
fighting power, is featured in the Horseradish-and-Mustard-Seed-
Crusted Bluefish, with the spicy herb crust complementing the
bluefish's rich flesh, and the Maple-Syrup-Glazed Maine Salmon

with Cortland Apple Wedges pairs flavorful salmon with local ingredients from that fish's domain.

Shellfish dishes abound along American's bays and bayous. The Maryland Crabcakes featured here are a classic — although sometimes it seems that there are more recipes for crabcakes than there are crabs in the ocean!

Until the time of the American Civil War, rice was king in the coastal areas of the Carolinas. Its popularity survives in dishes like the Carolina Shrimp Pilou (originally based on Near-Eastern pilafs) still served there. Further south and west, the Louisiana bayous are home to French-influenced seafood dishes. The Creole Soft-Shell Crab Doré and the Louisiana Crawfish Étouffée, a Cajun favorite, are tasty introductions to this unique area of American cuisine.

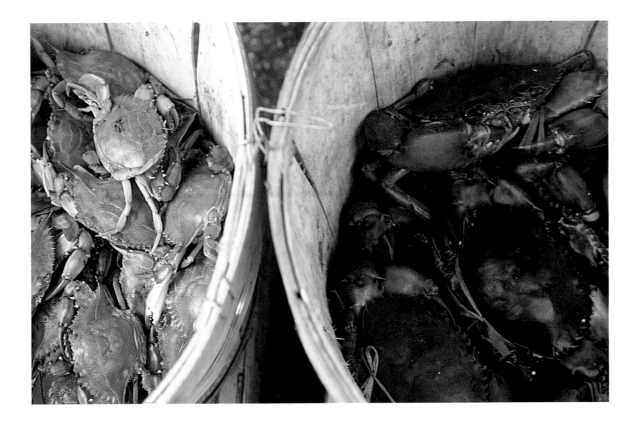

Maple Syrup-Glazed Maine Salmon with Cortland Apple Wedges

WILFRED BERIAU, CEC, AAC, CCE, CULINARY ARTS FACULTY,
SOUTHERN MAINE TECHNICAL COLLEGE, SOUTH PORTLAND, ME

With pure maple syrup and Cortland apples, this is truly a New England dish. Cortland apples are a modern American variety, bred from the Ben Davis and the McIntosh. They are semisweet, making them great cooking or eating apples. The richness of the salmon is contrasted by the slight acidity of these fruits of fall.

MAKES 4 SERVINGS

4 tablespoons butter

4 salmon fillets (about 6 ounces each)

½ cup all-purpose flour

Salt and freshly ground black pepper

1 tablespoon minced shallots

2 tablespoons dry white wine (such as Chardonnay or Sauvignon Blanc)

¼ cup pure maple syrup

2 tablespoons fresh lemon juice

3 Cortland apples, peeled, cored, and cut into wedges

3 scallions, thinly sliced

1 tablespoon chopped flat-leaf parsley

1 teaspoon grated lemon zest

3 tablespoons heavy cream

Heat a large skillet, preferably nonstick, over medium-high heat, 2 to 3 minutes. Add 1 tablespoon of the butter.

Dredge each of the salmon fillets in the flour and shake off the excess. Place them into the skillet, skin side down. Season with salt and pepper; cook until well browned, about 5 minutes. Turn and cook another 1 to 2 minutes; they should be slightly translucent in the center. Transfer to a large plate or platter and loosely cover to keep warm.

Wipe out the skillet, place it over medium heat, and add the remaining 3 tablespoons butter. When melted, add the shallots and cook, stirring, about 1 minute; add the wine. Cook until reduced by half, then add the maple syrup and lemon juice. Stir and simmer, 1 minute. Add the apples, scallions, parsley, and lemon zest to the pan. Stir to coat the apples with the sauce, and cook for 1 minute. Add the cream and cook until slightly thickened, about 2 minutes. Adjust the seasoning with salt and pepper.

Place the salmon fillets on serving plates and spoon the apple-syrup sauce over top.

Striped Bass Saltimbocca

VINCENT ALBERICI, AAC, EXECUTIVE CHEF,
ADAM'S MARK HOTEL, PHILADELPHIA, PA

Saltimbocca is a classic Italian dish, usually made with veal or chicken. The name means "jump in the mouth," which refers to the zesty flavor of the prosciutto used for wrapping the roulades. Making this dish with striped bass was my idea, as a way to update this old-style favorite.

MAKES 4 SERVINGS

12 ounces broccoli rabe, tough stems trimmed
and discarded

4 tablespoons olive oil

20 sage leaves

4 skinless striped bass fillets
(about 7 ounces each), butterflied

Salt and freshly ground black pepper

6 ounces thinly sliced prosciutto

1/2 cup Marsala wine

2 1/2 teaspoons minced garlic

2 ounces (1/4 cup) clam juice

8 ounces (1 cup) *demi-glace*
(available in gourmet markets)

1 teaspoon minced shallot

Preheat the oven to 350°F.

Bring a large pot of water to a boil. Generously salt the water and add the broccoli rabe, blanching it until it is bright green and tender, about 3 minutes. Drain and set aside.

Heat 2 tablespoons of the olive oil over medium heat in a medium skillet. When hot, add the sage leaves and fry them until crispy. Using tongs or a slotted spoon, transfer the leaves to a paper towel-lined plate.

Season the bass fillets with salt and pepper. Place 5 sage leaves in the center of each fillet, and roll in the form of a roulade. Neatly wrap pieces of the prosciutto around each fillet.

Place a large, ovenproof nonstick skillet over medium heat, 2 to 3 minutes. Add the wrapped bass and cook, turning until all sides are crispy. Transfer the pan to the oven and cook, 8 to 10 minutes. The fish should be firm to the touch.

Meanwhile, in a medium saucepan, add 1/2 teaspoon of the garlic and the Marsala and bring to a boil. Reduce the heat and simmer until reduced by half. Add the clam juice and *demi-glace,* and simmer again until reduced by half. Set aside.

In a large skillet over medium-high heat, add the remaining 2 tablespoons of oil, the remaining 2 teaspoons of garlic, and the shallots, and cook, stirring, until lightly browned, about 1 minute. Add the broccoli rabe, and season with salt and pepper. Cook, stirring, until the broccoli rabe is hot, about 3 minutes.

To serve, center the broccoli rabe on serving plates. Slice each of the roulades into four pieces, and transfer the slices to the serving plates. Pour the sauce around the plates and serve.

Brook Trout with Hazelnut Crust and Warm Asparagus Salad

FRITZ SONNENSCHMIDT, CMC, AAC, CULINARY DEAN,
THE CULINARY INSTITUTE OF AMERICA, HYDE PARK, NY

The inspiration for this recipe comes from the trout of the Snake River in Colorado, and the hazelnuts that grow nearby—a delicious meeting of the harvest of the land and the bounty of the river. You'll need only a few tablespoons of the asparagus stock—save the rest to make an asparagus soup.

MAKES 4 SERVINGS

8 trout fillets (about 6 ounces each)

Juice of 1 lemon

2 pounds asparagus, ends broken off or trimmed

4 tablespoons butter

1 tablespoon sugar

3 tablespoons tarragon or thyme vinegar

1 to 2 tablespoons minced fresh ginger

2 tablespoons chopped fresh chives

1 tablespoon chopped flat-leaf parsley

1/4 cup olive oil

Salt and freshly ground black pepper

1 1/2 cups finely chopped hazelnuts

1/2 cup unseasoned breadcrumbs

1/2 cup arrowroot or cornstarch

2 large eggs

2 tablespoons water

2 tablespoons canola oil

Place the fillets in a baking dish large enough to hold them in one layer. Drizzle with lemon juice. Cover and marinate, refrigerated, for at least 1 hour.

Meanwhile, using a sharp peeler, peel the stems of the asparagus. Set the asparagus spears aside. Place the peelings into a medium saucepan. Add 2 cups of water; bring to a boil. Lower the heat to simmer, and cook for 15 minutes. Strain the asparagus stock into a bowl and set aside. Discard the peelings.

To prepare the salad dressing, mix 2 to 3 tablespoons of the warm asparagus stock with 1 tablespoon butter and the sugar in a medium bowl. Add the vinegar, ginger, chives, and parsley, and stir to combine. Whisk in the olive oil and season with salt and pepper to taste. Set aside.

Cook the asparagus spears in boiling salted water until crisp-tender, 3 to 4 minutes. Drain and set aside. Cover loosely to keep warm.

Combine the hazelnuts with breadcrumbs and spread them on a plate. Place the arrowroot on a separate plate. In a medium bowl, lightly beat the eggs with the water. Set everything near the stove. (recipe continues on following page)

Brook Trout with Hazelnut Crust and Warm Asparagus Salad (continued)

Season a trout fillet with salt and pepper; dip it in the arrowroot to coat; shaking off any excess. Lay the fillet in the beaten eggs, then place it in the hazelnut/breadcrumb mixture, gently pressing to coat. Repeat with the remaining fillets, transferring them to a waxed paper-lined baking sheet as they are prepared.

Heat $1^1/_2$ tablespoons of the butter and 1 tablespoon of the canola oil in large sauté pan over medium-high heat. Add 4 fillets to the pan and cook until they are golden and crisp, about 2 minutes, then, using a spatula, turn and cook until just opaque in the center, about another 2 minutes. Repeat using the remaining butter and oil.

Portion the asparagus onto the serving plates and pour the vinaigrette over them. Add 2 trout fillets per plate. Serve immediately.

Horseradish-and-Mustard-Seed-Crusted Bluefish

VINCENT ALBERICI, AAC, EXECUTIVE CHEF,
ADAM'S MARK HOTEL, PHILADELPHIA, PA

Bluefish run from Cape Cod to Florida. Fresh-caught bluefish is succulent, sweet, and tender. They are a fairly high-fat fish, but the predominant fat is protective omega-3 fatty acid. Bluefish range from three to twenty pounds; the larger ones can have a rather intense flavor from their rich, oily flesh. I recommend three- to five-pound bluefish, which are milder, but still have enough flavor to hold up to this horseradish-and-mustard crust.

MAKES 4 SERVINGS

4 tablespoons olive oil

4 teaspoons crushed mustard seeds

2¹/₂ tablespoons grated fresh horseradish

¹/₂ teaspoon grated lemon zest

1 teaspoon chopped fresh chives

1 tablespoon fresh white breadcrumbs

4 bluefish fillets (about 7 ounces each)

Salt and fresh ground black pepper

In small bowl, prepare the crust; combine 2 tablespoons of the olive oil, the mustard seeds, horseradish, lemon zest, chives, and breadcrumbs and mix well. Season the fish fillets with salt and pepper. Pat the crust evenly on the flesh side of each filet.

Heat the remaining 2 tablespoons of the olive oil in a large nonstick skillet over medium-high heat. When the oil is wavy, place the fillets into the pan, flesh side down. Cook until a golden crust forms, about 2 minutes, then turn and cook another 2 to 3 minutes.

Flounder with Garden Vegetables en Papillote

KLAUS MULLER, CCE, AAC, DEAN, ACADEMY OF CULINARY ARTS, ATLANTIC CAPE COMMUNITY COLLEGE, MAYS LANDING, NJ

The term *en papillote* refers to a dish which is cooked in parchment paper in a hot oven, steaming the food in its own natural juices. I developed this recipe for a workshop sponsored by the Deborah Heart and Lung Center in Brown Mills, New Jersey. Using the day's catch of flounder and farm-fresh vegetables, I was able to show participants that healthy eating can be both easy and flavorful.

MAKES 4 SERVINGS

4 large pieces of parchment paper

1 to 2 teaspoons butter, at room temperature

Four 6-ounce flounder fillets

Salt and ground white pepper

1 tablespoon vegetable oil

2 celery stalks, cut into julienne

1 medium carrot, peeled, and cut into julienne

1 small onion, thinly sliced

4 ounces white mushrooms, stems removed, caps brushed clean, and thinly sliced

2 tablespoons soy sauce

2 tablespoons chopped flat-leaf parsley

4 lemon slices, peel removed

1/4 cup dry white wine, such as Chardonnay or Sauvignon Blanc

Preheat the oven to 400°F. Place a baking sheet in the oven to heat.

Cut the sheets of parchment paper into large heart shapes and rub lightly with butter.

Flatten the flounder fillets slightly, season with salt and pepper, and place each in the center of one side of one of the paper hearts. Set aside.

In a wok or large nonstick skillet, heat the oil over high heat, 2 to 3 minutes. Add the celery, carrot, and onion, and cook, stirring, about 1 minute. Stir in the mushrooms, soy sauce, and parsley and cook, stirring, another minute. Remove from the heat and quickly place some vegetables on top of each fish fillet.

Place a lemon slice on the top of the vegetables. Splash each portion with a little white wine. Fold the empty side of the paper over to cover the fish and vegetables and press the edges together to seal. Make a series of straight folds, one over the other, until you have a tight, heart-shaped package. Place them onto the preheated baking sheet and cook for 8 to 10 minutes, until the packages are inflated and aromatic. Serve the packages closed, allowing each diner to open his or hers at the table.

124 • AMERICAN HARVEST

PREPARING FISH
EN PAPILLOTE

In this variation of steaming, the fish and its accompanying ingredients are encased in parchment paper and cooked in a hot oven. The steam produced by the food's natural juices cooks the food.

The following steps are used to prepare foods to be cooked *en papillote*:

1. Cut a piece of parchment paper into a heart shape large enough to accomodate the fish and any additional ingredients (Fig. 1).

2. Butter or oil the parchment heart, and place the fish and its accompanying ingredients on one half of the parchment heart (Fig. 2).

3. Fold the empty half of the heart over the fish and fold and crimp the edges to seal the food in the parchment package (Fig. 3).

4. The fully-cooked fish in its package ready to be opened(Fig. 4).

1.

2.

3.

4.

Sautéed Salmon Cutlet with Sauerkraut

FRITZ SONNENSCHMIDT, CMC, AAC, CULINARY DEAN,
THE CULINARY INSTITUTE OF AMERICA, HYDE PARK, NY

The interaction of cultures is truly the American way, and this recipe is a perfect example. Salmon is a centerpiece of American cuisine, found in waters from coast to coast. Here it's combined with classic German sauerkraut to create an altogether new and enjoyable dish.

MAKES 4 SERVINGS

4 tablespoons olive oil

1 onion, diced

12 ounces prepared sauerkraut, rinsed

1½ cups chicken stock

¾ cup dry white wine, such as Chardonnay

1 apple, peeled, cored, and sliced

1 teaspoon juniper berries, optional

Pinch caraway seeds

1 bay leaf

1 potato, peeled and grated

Salt and freshly ground black pepper

3 shallots, finely diced

1 cup heavy cream

4 salmon fillets (about 6 ounces each),
    skin removed, if desired

Juice of 1 lemon

⅓ cup arrowroot or cornstarch

Heat 2 tablespoons of the olive oil in a medium sauté pan over medium heat. Add the onion and cook, stirring, 2 minutes. Add the sauerkraut, stock, ½ cup white wine, sliced apples, juniper berries, caraway seeds, and bay leaf. Cook, partially covered, stirring occasionally, until the sauerkraut softens, about 55 minutes. Stir in the grated potato, season with salt and pepper, and cook another 5 minutes. Set aside and keep warm.

Preheat the oven to 200°F.

In a medium saucepan, combine the remaining wine and the shallots. Bring to a boil and cook until reduced by two-thirds. Whisk in the cream and cook at a low boil until thick and syrupy, 5 to 7 minutes. Season with salt, transfer to a blender and whip to emulsify. Set aside and keep warm.

Place each salmon fillet between two sheets of plastic wrap, and flatten into cutlets by pressing gently. Set aside.

In a large nonstick skillet, heat 1 tablespoon of the olive oil over medium-high heat. Meanwhile, unwrap from the salmon and season with salt and pepper and the lemon juice. Lightly dust two of the cutlets with the arrowroot, shake off the excess, and place in the pan. Cook until lightly browned on both sides, about 5 minutes. Transfer the cutlets to an ovenproof platter and place in the oven. Heat the remaining tablespoon of olive oil in the skillet and cook the remaining cutlets.

Divide the sauerkraut among 4 plates. Lay the salmon over top and spoon the sauce over the salmon.

White Fish Stir Fry

RUDY GARCIA, CEC, AAC, EXECUTIVE CHEF, CULINARY ARTS,
LOS ANGELES MISSION COLLEGE, LOS ANGELES, CA

The heat of summer in Southern California offers a bounty of beautiful ingredients. My inspiration for this dish comes from the colorful produce available at the farmers' markets—golden beets, orange squash blossoms, and pencil-thin asparagus. Combined with delicate white fish, the result is a unique and light summer stir-fry. Try this recipe with a mild fish like *hoki* from Hawaii or halibut, and serve it over steamed white rice.

MAKES 8 SERVINGS

3 medium golden beets

1 pound asparagus

¼ cup peanut oil

1 tablespoon minced garlic

1 tablespoon crushed peppercorns (mixed colors)

2 pounds white fish, cut into 2-inch pieces

½ pound squash blossoms

1 tomato, diced

½ teaspoon curry powder

¼ cup apple cider

Salt and freshly ground black pepper

Place the beets in a small saucepan, add enough water to cover, and bring to a boil. Reduce the heat to maintain a slow boil, and cook until a knife can easily be inserted into the flesh, about 20 minutes. Drain. When cool enough to handle, peel and dice the beets. Set aside.

If asparagus is thick and tough, peel the stems. Otherwise, trim the tips, and cut the stems into 2-inch segments. Set the tips and stems aside separately.

Heat the oil in a large wok or sauté pan over high heat. When the oil is wavy, add the asparagus, garlic and peppercorns, and cook, stirring, about 1 minute. Add the fish, and continue to cook, stirring, 2 minutes. Add the remaining ingredients, including the reserved beets, and season with salt and pepper. Cook another 2 to 3 minutes, or until the fish is just done.

Sautéed Catfish with Marinated Lentils and Fried Horseradish

FRITZ SONNENSCHMIDT, CMC, AAC, CULINARY DEAN,
THE CULINARY INSTITUTE OF AMERICA, HYDE PARK, NY

Catfish has come a long way in American culinary circles. Once considered a food of the poor, catfish is now firmly established in contemporary cuisine, thanks in large part to the efforts of the many chefs who have featured it in their cooking. Frying the horseradish mellows its intensity and flavor, similar to what happens when garlic is roasted.

MAKES 4 SERVINGS

FOR THE VINAIGRETTE:

2 tablespoons sherry vinegar

$^1/_2$ teaspoon Dijon mustard

$^1/_4$ teaspoon salt

$^1/_3$ cup extra-virgin olive oil

Freshly ground black pepper

1 tablespoon chopped flat-leaf parsley

FOR THE CATFISH:

1$^1/_2$ cups cooked lentils, warm (see note)

2 tablespoons olive oil, plus more, as needed,
    to fry the horseradish

2-ounce piece fresh horseradish,
    peeled and thinly sliced

Salt and freshly ground black pepper

2 catfish fillets (about 8 ounces each),
    cut in half lengthwise on the diagonal

TO COOK THE LENTILS

In a small saucepan, bring 1$^3/_4$ cups of water or broth to a boil over medium-high heat. Stir in 1 cup lentils and a bay leaf, and season with salt and pepper. Reduce the heat to maintain a slow boil and cook, partially covered, until the lentils are tender, 35 to 40 minutes. Add a little more liquid during the cooking if necessary.

TO PREPARE THE VINAIGRETTE:

In a small bowl, whisk the vinegar, mustard, and salt. Slowly add the oil in a stream, whisking constantly, until all of the oil is used, and the dressing is emulsified. Whisk in the pepper and parsley and reserve.

TO PREPARE THE CATFISH:

In a medium bowl, combine the warm lentils with $^1/_4$ cup of the vinaigrette. Stir to combine and set aside.

Pour enough olive oil into a small skillet to come 1 inch up the sides. Heat over medium-high heat. When the oil is wavy, add the horseradish slices and fry, gently moving about and turning with a fork as they brown, until evenly browned and crispy. Using a skimmer or slotted spoon, remove the horseradish and transfer to a paper towel-lined plate. Pat dry and season with salt and pepper. Set aside.

Heat 2 tablespoons olive oil in a large skillet over medium-high heat. Season the pieces of catfish with salt and pepper, and place them into the skillet. Cook until lightly browned, 2 to 3 minutes, then turn and cook another 2 to 3 minutes, until opaque in the center.

To serve, spoon some lentils on each plate. Place a piece of catfish on the lentils and top with a few slices of the horseradish.

Whole Trout with Herbs and Foamy Butter Sauce

TIM RYAN, CMC, AAC, VICE PRESIDENT,
THE CULINARY INSTITUTE OF AMERICA, HYDE PARK, NY

The Hudson River, particularly between Newburgh and Albany, is rich with both common and rare species of fish, including largemouth and smallmouth bass, striped bass and shad, pickerel, northern pike, tiger muskies, and walleye. The Hudson's tributaries also make fine trout-fishing destinations, with none more outstanding than Esopus Creek. This clean, cold river, its source in the Catskill mountains, contains brook, brown, and rainbow trout.

MAKES 4 SERVINGS

4 whole boneless trout, butterflied

Juice of 2 lemons

4 sprigs fresh thyme

1/4 cup chopped flat-leaf parsley

2 tablespoons chopped fresh chives

2 tablespoons chopped fresh tarragon

2 teaspoons green peppercorns, packed in brine

1/2 teaspoon Worcestershire sauce

1 tablespoon olive oil

Salt and freshly ground black pepper

FOR THE BUTTER SAUCE:

1/4 cup dry white wine

1/4 cup white wine vinegar

1 tablespoon finely minced shallots

1 1/2 cups (3 sticks) unsalted butter, cut into small cubes

Salt and freshly ground black pepper

Place the trout in a casserole large enough to hold them in one layer. Drizzle with lemon juice, place a thyme sprig in the cavity of each trout. Close and evenly sprinkle the parsley, chives, tarragon, peppercorns, and Worcestershire sauce over each fish. Cover and marinate, refrigerated, for at least 1 hour.

Meanwhile, arrange the grill rack about 4 inches from the heat source and preheat the grill.

TO PREPARE THE BUTTER SAUCE:

In a small, nonreactive saucepan, combine the wine, vinegar, and shallots. Bring to a boil and cook until only 2 teaspoons of liquid remain. Reduce the heat to low, add the butter, a little at a time, and whisking constantly; add more butter only when the previous addition has been totally incorporated. When all the butter has been whipped in, season to taste with salt and pepper. Set aside and keep warm.

TO COOK THE TROUT:

Wipe any excess herb coating from the fish, then rub the exterior with olive oil. Season with salt and pepper, and place on the grill. Cook 6 minutes on the first side, turn, and cook another 4 to 6 minutes. To see if the fish is done, insert a paring knife carefully into the flesh. The flesh should pull away and appear moist. Serve topped with the Foamy Butter Sauce.

Tuna Savannah

ANDREW G. IANNACCHIONE, CEC, AAC, OWNER, HOSPITALITY REFERRALS/CONSULTANTS, CORPORATE CONSULTING CHEF, U.S. FOODSERVICE, BEDFORD, PA

Make this Southern-style recipe in the spring, when the waters along the Atlantic coast begin to warm, and the tuna migrate north. Tuna is the most popular fish in America but, unfortunately, most of it is sold in cans. Lately, fresh tuna has become very popular, perhaps because the steaks have a nice, firm texture that lends itself well to grilling.

MAKES 6 SERVINGS

4 tablespoons (1/2 stick) butter

2 shallots, peeled and thinly sliced

12 ounces large shrimp, peeled and deveined

1 cup coarsely chopped white button mushrooms

1 cup coarsely chopped portobello mushrooms

1/4 cup white wine

1 tablespoon freshly squeezed lemon juice

1 cup heavy cream

1 teaspoon fresh minced thyme

1 teaspoon fresh minced oregano

Salt and freshly ground black pepper

6 center-cut tuna steaks, such as yellowfin,
    1/2- to 3/4-inch thick (about 7 ounces each)

Preheat the grill.

Heat 2 tablespoons of the butter in a large skillet over medium heat. When hot, add the shallots and cook, stirring, until softened, 2 to 3 minutes. Add the shrimp and cook, stirring, 2 minutes. Add the white and portobello mushrooms. Cook, stirring, another 2 minutes. Add the wine and lemon juice. Simmer until the liquid has reduced by a third, then stir in the cream and the fresh herbs. Simmer until slightly thickened, about 4 minutes. Adjust the seasoning with salt and pepper and set aside.

Rub the tuna with the remaining 2 tablespoons butter and season with salt and pepper. Place them over the grill and cook to medium rare, about 3 minutes per side.

Spoon the shrimp-and-mushroom sauce onto 6 serving plates and lay the tuna steaks over the sauce.

Island-Style Swordfish

CARL H. WENDT, CEC, EXECUTIVE CHEF, QUALCOMM STADIUM,
VOLUME SERVICES AMERICA, SAN DIEGO, CA

Hawaiian flavors are easily found on many mainland menus. With their rich, meaty flavor, macadamia nuts are an excellent accent for the Eurasian Pacific cuisine of California. They add a toasty taste and a bit of crunch to grilled or broiled swordfish.

MAKES 6 SERVINGS

Six 6-ounce swordfish steaks

1 teaspoon vegetable oil

Salt and freshly ground black pepper

10 tablespoons unsalted butter

1 shallot, finely chopped

1 cup chopped macadamia nuts

1/2 cup dry white wine, such as Pinot Blanc
    or Pinot Grigio

Juice of 1 lemon

1/4 cup heavy cream

Three 1/2-inch-thick fresh pineapple slices, halved

Preheat the broiler. Place the swordfish steaks on a sheet pan lightly rubbed with the vegetable oil, season with salt and pepper, and place under the broiler. After 4 minutes, turn the steaks. Check doneness after 3 minutes—there should be only slight translucence in the center.

Meanwhile, in a medium sauté pan, heat 8 tablespoons butter over medium heat. When melted, add the shallots, and cook, stirring, until softened, about 3 minutes. Stir in the macadamia nuts, and cook another minute. Add the white wine. Simmer until the liquid is reduced by half. Add the lemon juice and cream and simmer, another 2 to 3 minutes. Set aside, partially covered, to keep warm.

Place the remaining 2 tablespoons butter in a medium skillet set over medium-high heat. Add the pineapple and cook until lightly browned, about 2 minutes; turn the pineapple slices and brown on the other side.

Place the steaks on serving plates, top each with a pineapple slice, and spoon the macadamia sauce over them.

Florida Seafood Pie

ANTHONY T. GILLETTE, CEC, CCE, AAC

I developed Florida Seafood Pie at the historic Bryan Homes Restaurant in South Florida. The early eighties were an exciting time on the Florida culinary scene. New Florida Cuisine is a fusion of local ingredients with the flavors of the Caribbean, as well as those of Spain and Morocco. My original recipe calls for gulf shrimp and golden crabmeat, but any shellfish may be substituted. Serve as a first course or an entrée.

MAKES 8 SERVINGS

¼ cup (½ stick) butter

1 small onion, diced

1 small green bell pepper, seeded and diced

1½ teaspoons minced garlic

8 ounces medium shrimp, peeled and deveined

4 ounces crabmeat

2 tablespoons chopped flat-leaf parsley

1 tablespoon dried basil

½ tablespoon dried oregano

¾ teaspoon salt

½ teaspoon freshly ground black pepper

1 large egg, lightly beaten

1 tablespoon mayonnaise

1¾ cups shredded Jarlsberg cheese

¾ cup unseasoned breadcrumbs

One prepared 9 inch pie shell

Preheat the oven to 350°F.

To prepare the filling, place the butter in a large skillet over medium heat. When melted, add the onion, green pepper, and garlic, and cook, stirring, until the vegetables soften, about 5 minutes. Add the shrimp and crab, and cook, stirring, until the shrimp turns pink, 2 to 3 minutes. Add the fresh and dried herbs; season with salt and pepper. Stir in the egg and mayonnaise; when well blended, remove from the heat, and mix in the cheese and breadcrumbs. Let cool slightly.

Transfer the filling to the prepared pie crust and spread it evenly, packing it down slightly. Place the pan in the oven, and bake until the filling and the crust are lightly browned, about 45 minutes. Let sit for about 10 minutes before slicing and serving.

Bay Scallops with Chive, Dill, and Tomato Vinaigrette

ROBERT G. WERTH, CEC, CCE, AAC,

FORMER DEPARTMENT CHAIRMAN AND FOUNDER, CULINARY TECHNOLOGY PROGRAM,

ASHEVILLE BUNCOMBE TECHNICAL COMMUNITY COLLEGE, ASHVILLE, NC

Scallops are an American favorite, harvested all along the American East Coast, down to the Gulf of Mexico. The bay scallops called for here are found in the area between Massachusetts and Long Island, New York.

MAKES 6 SERVINGS

$1/2$ cup olive oil

3 tablespoons freshly squeezed lemon juice

24 medium bay scallops

Salt and freshly ground black pepper

2 tablespoons unseasoned fresh breadcrumbs

1 pound fresh spinach, or other greens

12 red pear tomatoes

12 yellow pear tomatoes

2 tablespoons chopped fresh chives,
    plus 12 fresh chive sprigs

2 tablespoons chopped fresh dill

To prepare the marinade: Whisk together $1/4$ cup of the olive oil with the lemon juice in a medium bowl. Divide the marinade in half, setting half aside. Season the scallops with salt and pepper, and place in half the marinade, gently stirring or tossing to coat. Set aside for 10 minutes. Strain, and discard the marinade.

Heat the remaining $1/4$ cup olive oil in a large nonstick skillet over medium-high heat. Spread the breadcrumbs on a plate and coat both sides of the scallops, shaking off the excess. Place the scallops in the skillet and cook until they are lightly browned on both sides and spring back when gently probed, $1^1/2$ to 2 minutes per side.

Place the scallops on the outer rim of 6 serving plates. In the center of each plate, place a neat mound of the spinach. In a medium bowl, combine the red and yellow tomatoes, chopped chives, dill, and the reserved marinade, season with salt and pepper, and gently stir to combine. Place 2 red and 2 yellow tomatoes alternately between each scallop on each plate. Garnish with the chive sprigs.

Sautéed Bay Scallops with Pernod

ANTON FLORY, CMC, AAC, RETIRED CHEF INSTRUCTOR,
THE CULINARY INSTITUTE OF AMERICA, HYDE PARK, NY

Small, sweet bay scallops are generally found in the cold waters off the East Coast. You'll enjoy fishing them out of this creamy Pernod sauce. You can serve this dish with white rice, or over toasted bread.

MAKES 4 SERVINGS

1 cup light or heavy cream

2 tablespoons butter

1 tablespoon vegetable oil

2 tablespoons minced shallots

2 cloves garlic, minced

1¹/₂ cups sliced shiitake mushroom caps

2 cups fresh chopped watercress leaves

12 ounces bay scallops

2 tablespoons brandy

2 tablespoons Pernod

1 tablespoon *glace de viande*, optional, available in most gourmet food stores

Salt and freshly ground black pepper

1 tablespoon chopped fresh chives

Heat the cream in a small saucepan over medium heat. Bring to a boil, reduce the heat, and maintain a slow boil until the cream is reduced by half.

In a large skillet, heat the butter and oil over medium heat. When the butter is melted, add the shallots and cook, stirring, until translucent, about 2 minutes. Add the garlic and cook another minute, or until fragrant. Stir in the mushrooms and watercress. Cook, stirring often, until the mushrooms soften slightly, and their released liquid has mostly evaporated.

Turn the heat to medium-high, add the scallops, and cook, gently stirring, until they just begin to turn opaque, 1 to 2 minutes. Remove the pan from the heat and add the brandy. Carefully ignite the brandy with a match, preferably a long one, allowing it to flame until the alcohol burns off. Add the Pernod, reduced cream, and *glace de viande*, if using. Season with salt and pepper. Bring to a boil, then remove the saucepan from the heat, and serve garnished with a sprinkle of chives.

Lemon-Ginger Scallop and Shrimp Salad in Pineapple Cups

STAFFORD T. DE CAMBRA, CEC, CCE, AAC, SENIOR EXECUTIVE CHEF,
S.S. INDEPENDENCE, AMERICAN HAWAII CRUISES

This flavorful Hawaiian seafood salad has garnered numerous awards in culinary competitions. It blends the flavors lent by the Pacific Rim with Hawaii's abundance of fresh produce and seafood. I prefer to use local ingredients, like macadamia-nut oil, but this recipe will also work with the suggested substitutions. The lemon sauce may sound unfamiliar, but it is sold in Asian specialty markets everywhere.

MAKES 4 SERVINGS

FOR THE LEMON-GINGER DRESSING:

1 tablespoon sesame seeds

1 tablespoon black sesame seeds,
   or an additional tablespoon sesame seeds

10 ounces Chinese lemon sauce
   (available in Asian markets)

1/4 cup Chinese hoisin sauce

6 tablespoons Chinese rice wine vinegar

1/4 cup macadamia-nut oil (salad oil and
   1 tablespoon of dark roasted sesame oil
   may be substituted)

2 tablespoons drained, minced, pickled ginger

Salt and ground white pepper

FOR THE SEAFOOD SALAD:

2 pineapples (about 3 pounds each)

24 large sea scallops

24 large shrimp, peeled and deveined

1/2 cup chopped roasted peanuts

1/2 cup sliced water chestnuts, drained

8 sprigs fresh watercress,
   1/2 inch of stems trimmed

Place all the sesame seeds in a dry skillet just large enough to hold them in one layer. Set the skillet over medium heat and cook, shaking the pan frequently, until the seeds are lightly browned and begin to pop, about 5 minutes. Set aside.

TO MAKE THE DRESSING:

In a medium bowl, combine the lemon sauce, hoisin sauce, and rice vinegar. Add the macadamia-nut oil in a steady stream, whisking constantly to emulsify. Stir in the sesame seeds and pickled ginger; season to taste with salt and white pepper. Cover and place in the refrigerator.

Halve the pineapples horizontally, cut the ends off (about 1 inch below the flower and the bottom ends). The 4 pineapple pieces should sit steadily on a flat surface. Using a sharp paring knife, cut around the pineapple halves, close to the skin, to loosen the flesh. Using a spoon, scoop out the flesh without puncturing the bottom. Chop the fruit, reserving 1 1/2 cups. Set the pineapple shell aside.

Bring 2 quarts of salted water to a boil. Reduce the heat to maintain a slow boil. Add the shrimp and scallops. Cook 2 to 3 minutes, until the shrimp are pink and the scallops spring back slightly when touched. Drain into a colander, then place under cold running water to quickly cool. Drain again, and place in a large mixing bowl.

Add the chopped pineapple, roasted peanuts, and water chestnuts to the shrimp, and gently stir to combine. Pour the dressing into the bowl, and toss to evenly coat. Spoon the dressed seafood salad into the pineapple cups and garnish with watercress sprigs.

Scallops alla Stephanie

KLAUS MULLER, CCE, AAC, DEAN, ACADEMY OF CULINARY ARTS,
ATLANTIC CAPE COMMUNITY COLLEGE, MAYS LANDING, NJ

This recipe, named in honor of my wife Stephanie, earned the first place gold medal at the New Jersey Seafood Challenge, and carried New Jersey into the National Competition in Charleston, South Carolina, where it took the silver medal. The flavors of fresh sea scallops and fragrant, juicy tomatoes make this dish. If New Jersey tomatoes are not available, look for the most aromatic, red, summer variety that you can find.

MAKES 4 TO 6 SERVINGS

1½ pounds sea scallops

4 tablespoons butter, at room temperature

2 tablespoons all-purpose flour

1½ tablespoons minced shallots

6 ounces medium mushrooms, quartered

¾ cup fish stock (available frozen in some supermarkets and fresh in many fish markets)

½ cup dry white wine, such as Chardonnay or
Sauvignon Blanc

1 bay leaf

Salt

¾ cup heavy cream

1 teaspoon fresh chopped dill

3 ripe tomatoes, peeled (see Note),
seeded and cut into strips

If necessary, remove the tough adductor muscles from the scallops. Slice them in half crosswise and set aside.

In a small bowl, mix 2 tablespoons butter and the flour until smooth. Set aside.

Melt the remaining 2 tablespoons butter in a large sauté pan over medium heat. Add the shallots and cook, stirring, until translucent, about 2 minutes. Add the mushrooms and cook, stirring, another 2 minutes. Add the scallops, fish stock, wine, and bay leaf; season with salt. Simmer until the scallops turn opaque, 2 to 3 minutes: Strain the liquid into a medium saucepan. Remove and discard the bay leaf. Transfer the scallops and mushrooms to a medium bowl.

Whisk the butter and flour mixture, cream, and dill into the medium saucepan with the sauce and simmer, stirring constantly, until thickened, about 2 minutes. Stir in the scallops, mushroom, and tomatoes and cook 1 minute. Salt to taste and serve.

TO PEEL THE TOMATOES:

Place the tomatoes in a large pot of boiling water, about 1 minute. Remove, and let cool briefly. The skins will peel off easily.

Scallops Newburg

GERALD P. BONSEY, CEC, AAC, EXECUTIVE CHEF,
THE YORK HARBOR INN, YORK HARBOR, ME

Newburg is a rich dish that includes cream, butter, egg yolks, sherry, and chopped shellfish (typically lobster, crab, or shrimp). Scallops add an innovative touch to this traditional New England favorite.

MAKES 4 SERVINGS

4 tablespoons butter (1 tablespoon melted)

¼ cup sweet sherry

1 teaspoon paprika

¼ cup all-purpose flour

¾ cup light cream

Salt and ground white pepper

1½ pounds sea scallops

¾ cup unseasoned fresh breadcrumbs

Preheat the oven to 350°F.

To prepare the Newburg sauce, combine 2 tablespoons of the butter, the sherry, and paprika in the top of a double boiler. Place 2 to 3 inches of water in the bottom of the double boiler and bring to a boil. Reduce the heat to low, and set the top in the pot. Cook, stirring, until the butter is melted. Add the flour. Cook, stirring constantly, 1 minute. Whisk in the cream; season with salt and pepper. Simmer for 2 to 3 minutes, or until thickened and creamy. Remove from the heat. Set aside.

Grease a 3-quart casserole with 1 tablespoon of the butter. Place the scallops into the casserole and pour the Newburg sauce over them. In a small bowl, mix the breadcrumbs and the tablespoon of melted butter. Sprinkle this mixture over the casserole. Bake until lightly browned and bubbly, about 30 minutes.

Soft-Shell Crab Doré

GUNTER PREUSS, CEC, AAC, CHEF/OWNER,
BROUSSARD'S RESTAURANT, NEW ORLEANS, LA

Creole cooking combines the foods and flavors of the French, Spanish and African peoples who settled in the New Orleans area in the eighteenth century. For this dish I use the succulent soft-shell crabs that are caught in Lake Pontchartraw, Louisiana. They are in season during the spring and fall, and are harvested before they shed their edible, soft shell.

MAKES 6 SERVINGS

4 tablespoons butter

6 medium soft-shell crabs (about 4 ounces each), cleaned and dried

Salt and freshly ground black pepper

1 pound large shrimp, peeled and deveined

1/2 cup dry white wine, such as Chardonnay

1/4 cup minced shallots

1/4 cup thinly sliced scallions

1 cup sliced mushrooms

1/4 cup freshly squeezed lemon juice

1 clove garlic, minced

1/2 cup heavy cream

Heat 2 tablespoons of the butter in a large sauté pan over medium-high heat. When bubbling, season the crabs with salt and pepper, and add them to the pan in one layer (use two pans, or cook in batches, if necessary, to prevent crowding). Cook, turning once, until golden on both sides, about 6 minutes total.

Transfer the crabs to a platter. Add the shrimp and the wine to the sauté pan. Cook, stirring often, 2 to 3 minutes. Add the shallots, scallions, mushrooms, lemon juice, and garlic. Cook, stirring often, another 2 to 3 minutes. Stir in the cream; season with salt and pepper to taste. Simmer until the sauce thickens enough to coat the back of a spoon, about 3 minutes. Remove from the heat and stir in the remaining butter. Spoon some shrimp sauce on the center of each plate, and top with a sautéed crab.

CLEANING A SOFT-SHELL CRAB

Soft-shell crabs are not especially difficult to clean, once their various parts are identified. They are commonly prepared by sautéing or pan-frying, and the shell is usually eaten along with the meat. Following is the method for cleaning a soft-shell crab:

1. Peel back the pointed shell and scrape away the gill filament on each side (Fig. 1).

2. Cut off the head and carefully squeeze out the green bubble behind the eyes (Fig. 2).

3. Bend back the apron and twist to remove it and the intestinal vein at the same time (Fig. 3).

4. The cleaned soft shell crab ready for cooking (Fig. 4). The removed head, apron, and gill filaments, which are discarded, surround it.

1.

2.

3.

4.

Maryland Crabcakes

VICTOR A. L. GIELISSE, CMC, CHE, ASSOCIATE VICE PRESIDENT AND DEAN OF CULINARY, BAKING AND PASTRY STUDIES, THE CULINARY INSTITUTE OF AMERICA, HYDE PARK, NY

The bays that border the shores of Maryland are home to the blue crab. A little further inland, crab houses dominate the restaurant scene, offering pots of spicy steamed crabs served on newspaper-lined tables. When removed from the shell, the juicy, sweet meat makes heavenly cakes.

MAKES 4 SERVINGS

2 tablespoons olive oil

2 stalks celery, diced

1 large egg, lightly beaten

1 tablespoon mayonnaise

1 tablespoon minced fresh chives

1 tablespoon freshly squeezed lemon juice

3 drops Tabasco sauce

Pinch dry mustard

Pinch ground clove

Salt and freshly ground black pepper

Pinch cayenne pepper

1 pound blue crabmeat, any loose shells and cartilage removed and discarded (fresh or frozen lump crabmeat may be substituted)

$^1/_3$ cup toasted plain breadcrumbs

$^1/_4$ cup olive oil for frying, or a combination of canola oil and butter

In a medium skillet, cook the celery in 2 tablespoons olive oil over medium heat, stirring often, until slightly softened, about 5 minutes. Remove from the heat and let cool completely.

In a large bowl, combine the egg, mayonnaise, chives, lemon juice, Tabasco, mustard, and clove. Season with salt, black pepper and cayenne pepper. Stir to combine, then fold in the cooled celery and the crabmeat. Add the breadcrumbs and mix until just incorporated.

Form the mixture into 8 approximately 2-ounce patties.

Heat $^1/_4$ cup olive oil (or oil/butter combination) in a large skillet, preferably nonstick, over medium heat. When almost smoking, lay the patties in the pan, gently shaking and tilting the pan to evenly distribute the oil. Cook until golden on both sides. The total cooking time will be about 8 minutes.

Crab and Pasta Porcupine

BERT P. CUTINO, CEC, AAC, CHAIRMAN OF AAC 1995-1999,
CO-FOUNDER, THE SARDINE FACTORY RESTAURANT, MONTEREY, CA

Dungeness crab, representative of the Pacific Northwest's proud seafood heritage, is highly regarded around the world. It's been harvested all along the Pacific Coast since the late 1800s, from Monterey all the way up to Alaska. It is believed to be named after a small fishing village on the Strait of Juan de Fuca in Washington state. Weighing anywhere from 60 to 125 pounds and measuring 36 to 48 inches across, they are at their peak in December and January, however sizing has become an issue lately. The combination of pasta and crabmeat makes this recipe quite unique. When fried, the crabmeat takes on a porcupine effect, and that is where this recipe gets its name. Note that shrimp can be substituted for the crab in this recipe.

MAKES 6 SERVINGS

6 large eggs

1 pound cooked linguini (or substitute your favorite pasta)

2 cups crabmeat, preferably Dungeness

Salt and freshly ground black pepper to taste

1/2 cup chopped scallions

1 1/2 cups freshly grated Parmesan cheese, or substitute Asiago

3 cups unseasoned bread crumbs

Vegetable oil for deep frying

1 1/2 tablespoons salt

1 tablespoon garlic powder

1 tablespoon freshly ground black pepper

Salsa or other sauce for serving

Fresh dill for garnish

Preheat the oven to 350°F.

In a large bowl, lightly beat the eggs. Add the pasta, crabmeat, salt and pepper, scallions, and 1 cup of the cheese, and mix well. Portion the mixture into 12 pieces. Roll each portion in your hands to form and oval ball. Roll each ball in the breadcrumbs to coat well.

In a deep sauté pan, add vegetable oil to a depth of about 2 inches. Set over high heat until the oil reaches 350°F on a thermometer. Carefully add a few of the balls at a time, being careful not to overcrowd the pan which might cause the temperature of the oil to drop, and fry until golden brown. Transfer the balls to a baking dish and place in the oven just to heat through, about 10 minutes.

Serve the porcupine balls with your favorite salsa or other sauce, and garnish with a sprig of fresh dill.

Louisiana Crawfish Étouffée

JOHN FOLSE, AAC, GONZALES, LA

Étouffée, meaning to smother, is a popular cooking method in the Cajun country of Louisiana. Shrimp, crab, crawfish, meat, and game are often the star ingredients. Rice or pasta make a great base for these savory stews. A couple of dashes of hot sauce will adjust the heat to your taste.

MAKES 10 SERVINGS

½ cup (1 stick) butter

2 cups chopped onions

1 cup chopped celery

½ cup chopped green bell peppers

½ cup chopped red bell peppers

2 tablespoons minced garlic

½ cup diced tomatoes

2 bay leaves

3 pounds cleaned crawfish tails

½ cup tomato sauce

1 cup all-purpose flour

2 quarts fish stock or water

2 tablespoons sherry

2 bunches scallions, sliced

½ cup chopped flat-leaf parsley

2 tablespoons chopped fresh basil

1 tablespoons chopped fresh thyme

Salt and freshly ground black pepper

Hot sauce (optional)

In a 5-quart Dutch oven, melt the butter over medium-high heat. Add the onions, celery, peppers, and garlic and cook, stirring, until softened, about 5 minutes. Add the tomatoes and bay leaves, and cook 1 minute. Stir in half the crawfish tails and the tomato sauce. Using a wooden spoon, blend the flour into the mixture.

Slowly add the fish stock, a little at a time, stirring constantly, until well incorporated. Bring to a boil, then reduce the heat and simmer for 30 minutes, stirring occasionally. Add the remaining crawfish tails, sherry, scallions, parsley, basil, and thyme, and cook another 5 minutes. Season with salt and pepper, and hot sauce if desired.

Crawfish Florentine

ARTHUR E. KRETCHMAN, ACF, AAC, COOKBOOK AUTHOR,
INDUSTRY CONSULTANT (RETIRED), ATLANTA, GA

A convenience food that pleasantly surprised me was frozen, farm-raised crawfish tails. Until recently, it has been difficult to find sweet, succulent crawfish outside the Louisiana-Mississippi Basin, where they are abundant in bayous and streams. Now that crawfish are farmed commercially, cleaned and frozen, all of us can enjoy their scrumptious meat and the hours we save extracting it from their tails. In this recipe the slight bitterness of the spinach contrasts nicely with the sweetness of the crawfish. Serve this dish with rice or buttered pasta.

MAKES 6 SERVINGS

10-ounce package frozen spinach,
    thawed and drained

4 tablespoons (½ stick) butter

2 tablespoons minced onion

2 tablespoons diced uncooked bacon

3 tablespoons barbecue sauce

1 teaspoon curry powder

1 pound bag frozen, peeled, and deveined
    crawfish tails, thawed and drained

3 tablespoons shredded cheddar cheese
    (any sharpness)

1½ tablespoons freshly grated Parmesan cheese

½ cup unseasoned breadcrumbs

1 teaspoon garlic powder

Preheat the oven to 375°F. Squeeze any excess water from the spinach and set aside.

In a large skillet set over medium heat, melt 2 tablespoons of the butter. Add the onion and bacon and cook, stirring, 2 minutes. Add the barbecue sauce and curry powder and cook, stirring constantly, another 2 to 3 minutes. Transfer this mixture to a 1½-quart oval or round baking dish or casserole. Spread the crawfish over the top, then cover with the spinach and sprinkle with the cheddar and Parmesan cheeses. Set aside.

In a small skillet, heat the remaining 2 tablespoons butter over medium heat and stir in the breadcrumbs and garlic powder. Spread this mixture over the crawfish and spinach, cover, and bake for 25 minutes. Remove the cover and brown the top under the broiler, 1 to 3 minutes, depending on the closeness and intensity of the heat.

Black-Pepper Fettuccine with Sake-Clam Sauce

ANDREW G. IANNACCHIONE, CEC, AAC, OWNER, HOSPITALITY REFERRALS/CONSULTANTS, CORPORATE CONSULTING CHEF, U.S. FOODSERVICE, BEDFORD, PA

Fresh pasta was once difficult to find outside neighborhoods with a large Italian population, and flavored and colored pasta was even less common. Now, almost every supermarket sells fresh pasta in the refrigerator case. You might have to search for the black-pepper fettuccine called for in this recipe, but you can use the plain variety if necessary. This dish reflects a fusion of Italian and Japanese cooking—classical Italian white-clam sauce is made with Japanese *sake* wine instead of the traditional Italian white wine.

MAKES 4 SERVINGS

10 ounces fresh black-pepper fettuccine
(plain fettuccine may be substituted)

1 tablespoon extra-virgin olive oil

4 anchovy fillets

1/4 cup minced onion

1 to 2 tablespoons minced garlic

12 ounces chopped clams with juice

1 cup Japanese *sake* wine

2 tablespoons capers, drained and rinsed

8 calamata olives, pitted

2 tablespoons chopped flat-leaf parsley

1/4 cup freshly grated Pecorino Romano cheese

4 basil flowers to garnish, optional

Bring a large pot of water to a boil. Generously salt, and add the fettuccine. Cook according to package instructions, until *al dente*, and drain.

While the pasta cooks, heat the olive oil in a medium skillet over medium heat. Add the anchovies, onions, and garlic, and cook, stirring, until the anchovy fillets disintegrate into a paste. Add the clams and their juice, and simmer until liquid is reduced by one-quarter. Add the sake, capers, olives, and parsley, and simmer, stirring often, 3 minutes.

Add the cooked pasta to the skillet and cook, tossing or stirring, until the pasta is hot and evenly coated. Using tongs, place the fettuccine in a pasta bowl. Pour the sake sauce over top, sprinkle with the cheese, and garnish with the basil, if using. Serve immediately.

Five-Flavored Prawns

MARTIN YAN, AAC, YAN CAN COOK, INC.

Depending on which side of the Pacific—or which side of the Mississippi, for that matter—you call home, prawns and shrimp can be very different things indeed. Generally, Chinese cooks are fond of prawns, if for no other reason than they are normally larger and, we think, tastier. If you can't get your hands on prawns, go ahead and use fresh, plump shrimp—the dish will be just as delicious.

MAKES 4 SERVINGS

FOR THE MARINADE:

1 tablespoon Chinese rice wine

1 tablespoon cornstarch

$1/2$ teaspoon salt

1 pound jumbo prawns, shelled and deveined, tails intact

FOR THE SAUCE:

$1/4$ cup Chinese rice vinegar

$1/4$ cup chicken broth

1 tablespoon oyster sauce

2 teaspoons sesame oil

1 tablespoon sugar

$1/4$ teaspoon Chinese five-spice powder

2 tablespoons peanut oil

8 small dried chiles

4 teaspoons minced garlic

$1/2$ red bell pepper, cut into 1-inch squares

2 teaspoons cornstarch dissolved in 1 tablespoon water

TO PREPARE THE MARINADE:

In a medium bowl, combine the rice wine, cornstarch, and salt. Add the prawns, turning to coat. Set aside for 10 minutes.

TO PREPARE THE SAUCE:

In another bowl, stir together the rice vinegar, chicken broth, oyster sauce, sesame oil, sugar, and Chinese five-spice powder. Set aside.

TO COMPLETE THE DISH:

Place a wok over high heat. When hot, add 1 tablespoon of the peanut oil, swirling to coat the bottom and sides. Add the chiles and cook, stirring, until fragrant, about 10 seconds. Drain the prawns from the marinade, add to the wok, and stir-fry until they turn pink, about 2 minutes. Transfer the chiles and the prawns to a plate.

Add remaining peanut oil to the wok, add the garlic and cook, stirring, until fragrant, about 10 seconds. Add the bell pepper, and stir-fry, $1^{1}/2$ to 2 minutes. Return the prawns and their juices to the pan. Add the sauce and bring to a boil. Stir in the cornstarch and cook, 2 minutes, or until thickened.

Carolina Shrimp Pilou

ROBERT E. BOYTER SR., CEC, AAC

The story of how rice was introduced to this country varies. According to one source, in 1680, rice was smuggled into Charleston, South Carolina to D. Henry Woodard, who planted it, and found that it flourished. By the eighteenth century, it was such an important crop that it was used for currency and referred to as Carolina Gold. The Carolina crops never recovered from the devastation caused by the Civil War and today, Arkansas, California, Louisiana, Mississippi, Missouri, and Texas produce the bulk of the rice crop in America.

MAKES 6 SERVINGS

8 slices uncooked bacon

1 large onion, minced

2 red bell peppers, cored, seeded, and diced

4 scallions, green portions chopped

1 clove garlic, minced

3 cups chicken broth

1 1/2 cups long-grain white rice

One 28-ounce can diced tomatoes

2 teaspoons Worcestershire sauce

1 teaspoon ground mace

Salt and cayenne pepper

2 pounds medium shrimp, peeled and deveined

2 tablespoons chopped flat-leaf parsley

Preheat the oven to 350°F.

In a heavy 3-quart Dutch oven or pot with a cover, cook the bacon over medium heat, turning occasionally, until the fat is rendered and the strips are crispy, about 10 minutes. Remove the pan from the heat, and transfer the bacon to a paper towel-lined plate, leaving the fat in the pan. When the bacon is cool enough to handle, crumble and set aside.

Place the Dutch oven over medium heat; add the onion and the bell peppers. Cook, stirring often, until tender, about 5 minutes. Add the scallions and garlic. Stir, cook another minute; add the broth, rice, tomatoes, Worcestershire sauce, and mace. Season with salt and cayenne, and stir to combine. Bring to a boil, stir in the shrimp and bacon, cover and transfer to the oven. After 15 minutes, remove from the oven and fluff the rice with a fork. Serve sprinkled with parsley.

Stuffed Calamari Sicilian-Style

JOSEPH B. RIVAS, CEC, AAC, FORMER EXECUTIVE CHEF,
GREEN HILLS GOLF AND COUNTRY CLUB, MILLBRAE, CA

San Francisco is best known in culinary circles for two things—its very large Little Italy (and all of its wonderful restaurants), and the availability of high-quality seafood. Squid is only available frozen in many parts of the country, but you should be able to find it fresh in North Beach. Remember the key to cooking squid: Do not overcook it, otherwise it will become tough. Serve this classic Italian-American dish over rice or spaghetti.

MAKES 6 SERVINGS

2 tablespoons olive oil

3 cups crushed Italian-style tomatoes

1 clove garlic, thickly sliced

2 cups fresh breadcrumbs

1 cup freshly grated Pecorino Romano cheese

3 large eggs, lightly beaten

1 tablespoon chopped flat-leaf parsley

1 tablespoon chopped fresh basil

Salt and freshly ground black pepper

6 large squid bodies, cleaned

Heat the olive oil and garlic in a medium sauté pan set over medium heat. Cook, stirring, 1 to 2 minutes; do not let the garlic brown. Add the tomatoes, and when the mixture begins to boil, adjust the heat so that it gently simmers.

Meanwhile, in a medium bowl, combine the breadcrumbs, Romano cheese, eggs, parsley, and basil; season with salt and pepper. Mix until well combined.

Spoon the filling into the tubes of the squid, and secure end closed with a toothpick. Place them into the simmering sauce and cook, turning occasionally, 12 minutes. Do not overcook the calamari, as they will toughen.

CLEANING SQUID

Squid are not difficult to prepare, but they do need some advance preparation to remove the ink sac and quill. If desired, the ink sac can be saved and used to prepare various dishes. The method to clean and prepare a squid for cooking is as follows:

1. Pull the mantle and tentacles apart under running water (Fig. 1).

2. Pull off the skin from the mantle (Fig. 2).

3. Pull out the quill from the mantle (Fig. 3).

4. Cut the tentacles away from the head by cutting just above the eye (Fig. 4). The ink sac can be removed and reserved, if desired.

5. Open out the tentacles and pull out the beak (Fig. 5). You can remove the beak by popping it out with your fingers or the tip of a knife.

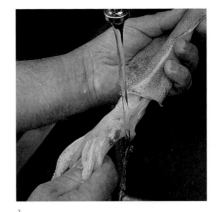

1.

2.

3.

4.

5.

CHAPTER SIX

Desserts

American Classics, Old and New,

Perfect Endings for Any Meal

A MERICA HAS LONG HAD A COLLECTIVE SWEET tooth. As recently as fifty years ago, the dessert chapter was usually the largest one in any American cookbook. While our tastes may have become more sophisticated in recent years, who doesn't appreciate a delicious dessert to top off a perfect meal?

With the recent trend of looking to the past for "comfort foods"—those simple yet uniquely-satisfying foods we remember from our childhood—many traditional American desserts are making a comeback, sometimes in surprising new interpretations. Peanuts and chocolate, a favorite flavor combination, are highlighted in the Norfolk Peanut Butter Cheesecake with Chocolate Crust, which also pays tribute to the cocoa and peanut trades of Norfolk, Virginia. Bread pudding has made a comeback on restaurant menus, and the Chocolate Hershey Bar Bread

Pudding and Caramelized Bread Pudding with Walnuts, Banana, and Ginger offer two delicious variations on this homey dessert. Baked Golden Delicious Apples are a dessert tradition that originated in Tuscany, but are made here with a native American apple variety. And the Spring Strawberry Rhubarb Sorbet offers the unique taste of a spring rhubarb variety in a refreshing frozen dessert.

When the largest section of older American cookbooks was devoted to desserts, the largest proportion of those desserts was pie, and the Strawberry-Pineapple Pie, with its refreshing fruit flavors, and the Blue Cheese, Pear, and Port Pie, taking a classic English after-dinner combination to new heights, are two sophisticated additions to the American pie tradition.

Norfolk Peanut Butter Cheesecake with Chocolate Crust

LISA BREFERE, CEC, AAC, EXECUTIVE CHEF,
FLIK INTERNATIONAL AT BEAR STEARNS, NEW YORK, NY

The combination of peanuts and chocolate is an American original. Ships carrying cocoa beans frequently dock at the ports in Norfolk, Virginia, where the aroma of the roasting beans perfumes the air. Virginia is also one of the largest peanut-producing states. This rich dessert is named in honor of the city that facilitates the blending of these ingredients.

MAKES ONE 10-INCH CAKE, APPROXIMATELY 16 SERVINGS

8 ounces semisweet chocolate,
　　cut into small pieces

2 tablespoons unsalted butter

3 large egg yolks

1/3 cup sugar

2 large egg whites

14 ounces cream cheese, softened

1 cup confectioners' sugar

1 1/2 cups creamy peanut butter

1/4 teaspoon unflavored gelatin

1/4 cup Kahlúa

2 cups heavy cream

Preheat the oven to 350°F.

Coat a 10-inch cake pan with cooking spray and line the bottom with parchment paper; spray the top of the parchment paper and set aside.

Place 2 inches of water in the bottom of a double boiler, bring to a boil, then reduce the heat so that the mixture steams. Add the chocolate and butter to the top of the double boiler and place it over the bottom. Cook, stirring constantly, until the butter and the chocolate are melted and well combined. Remove from the heat; set aside to cool slightly.

In a medium bowl, using a hand-held mixer or a wire whisk, beat the egg yolks with the sugar until they are pale and fluffy, 8 to 10 minutes. Set aside.

In the bowl of a standing mixer or in large bowl using a hand-held mixer (if using the same mixer as was used for the egg yolks, make sure the beaters are thoroughly cleaned and dried), whip the egg whites until they form soft peaks. Set aside.

Gradually, add the warm chocolate to the egg yolk, stirring constantly. Add this mixture to the egg whites, folding it in with a rubber spatula just until well combined. Transfer to the prepared cake pan and spread evenly. Bake, 10 to 15 minutes, until it's set and firm (it should feel like a cooked quiche). Transfer to a baking rack to cool.

In a mixing bowl, beat the cream cheese with the confectioner's sugar, with a paddle attachment if available, until light and fluffy. Add the peanut butter, and mix until incorporated.

In a metal bowl or in the top half of a double boiler, sprinkle the gelatin over the Kahlúa and let sit for 5 minutes. Warm the Kahlúa over a pan of simmering water in a double boiler, stirring, until dissolved, and no strands are visible. Pour the heated Kahlúa mixture into the peanut butter mixture in a slow steady stream, and set aside.

In a clean bowl, whip the heavy cream to fairly soft peaks. Fold the whipped cream into the peanut butter mixture, then pour over the baked chocolate layer. Allow the cake to set for 2 hours, or overnight in the refrigerator, before serving.

Chocolate Hershey Bar Bread Pudding

JOHNNY RIVERS, CEC, AAC, OWNER,
JOHNNY RIVER'S SMOKEHOUSE & BBQ CO., ORLANDO, FL

The cooking of the American South has a long tradition of not letting any food go to waste. Bread pudding was created to make use of old, stale bread, though these days, we usually have to toast our bread to give it the proper texture. When I was a child, my mother used to make this bread pudding with pineapples or bananas, two Floridian favorites, and Hershey chocolate, a special treat. I've updated the recipe a bit for my restaurant, adding pecans, another Southern specialty. There isn't any fruit in this recipe, but I encourage you to have fun with it, and add some bananas or whatever fruit you enjoy most.

MAKES 4 SERVINGS

2 cups milk

4 large egg yolks

$1/2$ cup plus 2 tablespoons sugar

6 teaspoons ground cinnamon

2 teaspoons vanilla extract

6 cups bite-sized pieces white bread

$1/4$ cup ($1/2$ stick) unsalted butter

6 ounces Hershey's chocolate,
   broken into small pieces

$1/2$ cup chopped pecans

1 cup Vanilla-Bean Bourbon Sauce (recipe follows)

$3/4$ cup Hershey's Chocolate Syrup

VANILLA-BEAN BOURBON SAUCE:

1 tablespoon cornstarch

2 tablespoons bourbon

1 cup milk

1 large egg yolk

$1/4$ cup sugar

1 teaspoon vanilla extract

$1/4$ teaspoon salt

Preheat the oven to 350°F.

Prepare a custard: Whisk together the milk, egg yolks, $1/2$ cup sugar, cinnamon, and vanilla in a large bowl. Set aside.

Spread the bread in a single layer on a large baking pan with sides. Place the butter in a small saucepan over medium heat. When melted, drizzle the butter over the bread and toss or stir to evenly coat. Place the pan into the oven and bake until lightly browned, about 15 minutes. Keep the oven temperature at 350°F. Transfer the bread to the bowl with the custard and gently stir to saturate all pieces. Set aside 2 to 3 minutes.

Spray a 10-inch cast-iron skillet with cooking spray. Line the bottom of the skillet with parchment or baking paper. Spoon half of the bread/custard mixture on top, spreading in an even layer. Sprinkle the chocolate over the bread, then top with the remaining soaked bread. Sprinkle the pecans and remaining sugar on top. Bake for 30 minutes. Serve warm with Vanilla Bean Bourbon Sauce and Hershey's Chocolate syrup drizzled on top.

TO MAKE THE VANILLA-BEAN BOURBON SAUCE:

In a small bowl, stir together the cornstarch and bourbon. In a medium, heavy-bottomed saucepan, whisk together the milk, egg yolk, sugar, vanilla, and salt. Place the pan over medium heat and bring the mixture to a boil, stirring constantly. Reduce the heat to low, add the cornstarch mixture and cook, whisking constantly, for another minute, or until thickened. Keep warm.

Caramelized Bread Pudding with Walnuts, Banana, and Ginger

LISA BREFERE, CEC, AAC, EXECUTIVE CHEF,
FLIK INTERNATIONAL AT BEAR STEARNS, NEW YORK, NY

Bread pudding is considered comfort food by many Americans. This simple dessert can be made quickly by making a custard and utilizing scraps of leftover bread. I substituted leftover Danish pastry for the bread, and topped the dish with caramelized bananas to add some flair.

MAKES 8 SERVINGS

5 tablespoons unsalted butter

1½ cups coarsely chopped walnuts

1 pound leftover Danish pastry,
    such as almond paste, cheese or fruit filled,
    cut into 1-inch cubes

3 bananas, peeled and cut into ⅛-inch-thick slices

2 cups heavy cream

⅓ cup plus 2 tablespoons sugar

1 tablespoon minced fresh ginger

1 teaspoon pure vanilla extract

3 large eggs, lightly beaten

Preheat the oven to 350°F.

Rub eight 6-ounce ramekins, or a 1½- to 2-quart ovenproof glass or ceramic baking dish, with 1 tablespoon butter.

Place the walnuts in a dry skillet just large enough to hold them in one layer. Set the skillet over medium heat and cook, shaking the pan frequently, until the walnuts are fragrant and lightly browned, about 5 minutes. Let cool briefly.

In a large bowl, combine the Danish pastry, two-thirds of the bananas, and the walnuts, and stir to incorporate. Set aside.

Place the cream in a medium saucepan, and whisk in ⅓ cup sugar, the ginger, and vanilla and turn the heat to medium. Cook just until it begins to steam. Remove from the heat and let cool slightly.

Add a little of the cream to the lightly beaten eggs, whisking constantly, to temper the eggs. Add the egg mixture to the cream, stirring constantly. Pour the custard into the bowl with the Danish and stir to combine. Divide among the prepared ramekins or place in baking dish. Set the ramekins into a baking pan and add hot water, to within about 1½ inches of the top of the ramekins. Bake until the mixture just sets, about 25 minutes, or about 10 minutes longer if you're using a baking dish.

Meanwhile, caramelize the remaining banana slices. Heat the remaining 4 tablespoons butter in a medium skillet set over medium-high heat. When hot, add the banana slices to the skillet and cook, turning frequently, until golden, about 4 minutes. Sprinkle with the remaining 2 tablespoons of sugar and cook 1 minute. Transfer to a plate lined with baking paper and let cool, to crisp. Serve the pudding with caramelized banana slices spooned over the top.

Baked Golden Delicious Apples

HARRY BROCKWELL, CEC, AAC, OCEANSIDE CATERERS, WESTLAKE VILLAGE, CA

I discovered this recipe in Tuscany; it was the first time I'd encountered the Golden Delicious apple used in a dessert— normally you'd use a crisp apple like a Granny Smith for baking. The Golden Delicious apple is delicate, so, when you remove the core, the wine and sugar easily permeate the flesh. The Grand Marnier adds a wonderful burst of flavor. Try serving this dish with raspberries, or, for richer tastes, try it with crème fraiche, whipped cream, or even rich vanilla ice cream.

MAKES 6 SERVINGS

6 Golden Delicious apples

6 tablespoons golden raisins

3 cups dry white wine, such as Chardonnay or
　Sauvignon Blanc

6 tablespoons sugar

6 tablespoons Grand Marnier

1 cup fresh raspberries for garnish

Preheat the oven to 325°F.

Core the apples, but do not cut all the way through to the bottom. Scoop out the core working from the top. Place the cored apples into a roasting pan just large enough to hold them. Add a tablespoon of raisins to the center well of each apple. In a small bowl, mix the wine, sugar, and 4 tablespoons of the Grand Marnier. Spoon this mixture into the well with the raisins; when full, pour the remaining liquid over the exterior of the apples and into the bottom of the pan.

Bake until the apples are tender but still hold their shape, 50 to 60 minutes. Serve garnished with fresh raspberries and a splash of the remaining Grand Marnier.

Strawberry Pineapple Pie

WILFRED BERIAU, CEC, AAC, CCE, CULINARY ARTS FACULTY,
SOUTHERN MAINE TECHNICAL COLLEGE, SOUTH PORTLAND, ME

July is strawberry month in Maine and it is celebrated with all kinds of events, including the Strawberry Festival in Oquossoc. A traditional Maine Fourth of July menu would include salmon, served with new potatoes, fresh peas, cream, and butter. And you'd finish it off with a classic dessert like strawberry shortcake. I thought it would be fun to combine strawberries with another American favorite, pineapple, to create this summertime pie.

MAKES 6 TO 8 SERVINGS

FOR THE PIE SHELL:

1 1/3 cups all-purpose flour

1 teaspoon sugar

1/4 teaspoon salt

1/8 teaspoon baking powder

1/2 cup (1 stick) unsalted butter, cold, cut into small cubes

2 to 3 tablespoons ice water

FOR THE FILLING:

2 cups diced fresh pineapple

3 cups diced fresh strawberries

1 1/3 cups sugar

1/4 cup cornstarch

1/2 cup all-purpose flour

1/3 cup cold unsalted butter, cut into pieces

1/3 cup packaged sweetened coconut

TO PREPARE THE PIE SHELL:

In a food processor fitted with the metal blade, process the flour, sugar, salt, and baking powder to combine, 5 seconds. Add the butter cubes to the flour and process for about 15 seconds, or until the mixture resembles coarse meal.

Add no more than 2 tablespoons ice water and pulse a few times. Pinch a small amount of the mixture between your fingers. If it does not hold together, add the remaining tablespoon of water and pulse again. The mixture should look crumbly and will not hold together without being pinched. Using your hands, gather the dough together in a ball. Wrap with plastic wrap, flatten it into a disc, and refrigerate for at least 30 minutes, preferably overnight.

Preheat the oven to 350°F.

To roll, unwrap the dough and place it on a lightly flour-dusted flat surface. Roll, pressing lightly, from the center out, dusting with flour, as necessary, on and under the dough to prevent sticking. Continue to roll until it is at least 10 inches in diameter and less than 1/4-inch thick.

Center the dough in a 9-inch pie plate. Press the dough to the bottom and around the sides. Trim, leaving a 1/4- to 1/2-inch reserve all the way around. Crimp the dough between two fingers to form a decorative crust. Place a piece of foil wrap on the bottom of the dough and fill with dried beans or pie weights. Prebake the crust, 10 to 12 minutes. Set aside to cool on a wire rack.

In a large bowl, combine the pineapple, strawberries, 1 cup of the sugar, and the cornstarch. Stir to combine, then transfer the mixture to the prebaked crust.

In a small bowl, mix the flour with the remaining $1/3$ cup sugar. Using two knifes, cut the butter pieces into the flour. Evenly distribute this crumb topping over the fruit; sprinkle with coconut. Bake 35 minutes. Serve slightly warm with a dollop of whipped cream or ice cream.

PREPARING A
PIE CRUST

1. Use a rolling pin to roll the pie crust dough in one direction on a diagonal, on a lightly flour-dusted flat surface. (Fig. 1)

2. Switch hands and roll in the opposite direction. (Fig. 2) Dust with flour as necessary to prevent the dough from sticking.

3. Carefully fold the pie crust dough and transfer from the work surface to the pie plate. (Fig.3)

4. Use a scrap of dough to gently press the dough into the corners of the pie plate. (Fig. 4)

1.

2.

3.

4.

Blue Cheese, Pear, and Port Pie

BARBARA SANDERS, MS, CEC, AAC, CULINARY INSTRUCTOR/CONSULTANT, MONROE, NH

Fruit and blue cheese is a popular dessert combination in Europe, and port is a wonderful accompaniment. I wanted to create a dessert that combined all those flavors. I sweetened it with maple syrup instead of sugar to add a distinctly American twist.

MAKES 8 SERVINGS

FOR THE CRUST:

1⅓ cups all-purpose flour, plus extra for dusting

3 teaspoons sugar

1 tablespoon baking powder

Pinch salt

1½ tablespoons butter, cold, cut into small cubes

⅓ cup part-skim ricotta

2 tablespoons skim milk

1 large egg white

1 teaspoon maple syrup

FOR THE PORT WINE SAUCE:

5 ounces (about 1⅓ cups) crumbled blue cheese

1 cup apple juice

½ cup port wine

2 tablespoons cornstarch

1 tablespoon sugar

1 tablespoon maple syrup

3 Anjou pears, cored and diced

1 Granny Smith apple, cored and diced

In a food processor fitted with the metal blade, process the flour, sugar, baking powder, and salt to combine, 5 seconds. Add the butter cubes to the flour and process, about 15 seconds, or until the mixture resembles coarse meal. Add the ricotta, skim milk, egg white, and maple syrup, and pulse a few times.

Using your hands, gather the dough together in a ball. Wrap the dough with plastic wrap, flatten it into a disc, and refrigerate for at least 30 minutes, preferably overnight.

Divide the dough in half, and roll out each half, separately, on a surface dusted generously with flour, pressing lightly, from the center out, and dusting the dough and the rolling pin with flour as necessary to prevent sticking. (This dough will be quite moist.) Roll the piece of dough that will be the bottom crust to at least 10 inches in diameter and less than ¼ inch thick. The top crust can be slightly smaller; after the top crust has been rolled, place it between two sheets of plastic wrap and refrigerate.

Center the larger piece of dough in a 9-inch pie plate. Press the dough to the bottom and the sides and trim the dough, leaving a ¼- to ½-inch reserve all the way around. Refrigerate for 5 to 10 minutes.

Preheat the oven to 350°F.

TO PREPARE THE SAUCE:

Combine the blue cheese, apple juice, port, cornstarch, sugar, and maple syrup in the work bowl of a food processor or blender. Puree until smooth. Transfer the mixture to a small saucepan, and cook over medium heat, stirring often, until thickened, about 10 minutes. Set aside to cool slightly.

Place the diced pears and apples on the bottom of the prepared pie crust. Pour the sauce over the fruit, and center the top crust over the pie. Crimp the edges of the top and bottom crusts together to seal. Bake, 35 minutes, until golden brown.

Gluehwein Soufflé

ANTON FLORY, CMC, AAC, RETIRED CHEF INSTRUCTOR,
THE CULINARY INSTITUTE OF AMERICA, HYDE PARK, NY

Gluehwein is a traditional Austrian or Bavarian spiced mulled wine, usually made with cinnamon and cloves, and served warm during the colder months. Here, the flavors of *gluehwein* combine with fluffy meringues and currant jelly for a savory dessert.

MAKES 4 SERVINGS

¹/₂ cup (1 stick) unsalted butter

8 thick slices day-old Austrian Semmel bread, or any kind of firm white bread

1¹/₂ cups dry but mellow and slightly fruity red wine, such as Dolcetto d'Alba or Merlot

³/₄ cup sugar

12 whole cloves

1 large cinnamon stick

1¹/₂ teaspoons arrowroot or cornstarch

¹/₂ cup currant jelly

3 large eggs, separated

3 tablespoons all-purpose flour, sifted

1 tablespoon vanilla extract

2 tablespoons confectioner's sugar

Preheat the oven to 375°F.

Heat the butter in a large sauté pan over medium heat. When bubbling, place the bread slices into the pan in one layer and cook until golden brown on both sides, about 5 minutes total. Transfer the bread slices to a plate and let cool slightly.

TO PREPARE THE MULLED WINE:

Combine the wine, ¹/₂ cup of the sugar, the cloves, and cinnamon stick in a medium saucepan. Bring to a boil, then reduce the heat and simmer 10 minutes, to blend the flavors. In a small bowl, mix the arrowroot with 2 tablespoons water, then stir this mixture into the pan. Cook another 2 to 3 minutes, until the wine is light and syrupy. Remove from the heat and set aside.

TO COMPLETE THE DESSERT:

Spread the currant jelly over the bread slices and arrange them in one layer in a 10 x 10-inch glass baking dish. Pour two-thirds of the mulled wine evenly over the bread slices and set aside.

In a small bowl, lightly beat the egg yolks. Set aside. In a standing mixer or in a large bowl using a hand-held mixer, beat the egg whites with the remaining ¹/₄ cup sugar to soft peaks. Using a rubber spatula, fold the egg yolks, flour, and vanilla into the egg whites. Evenly spoon a neat mound of this meringue over each bread slice, making sure each slice is covered. Transfer the pan to the oven and bake, 10 minutes, or until the meringue is lightly browned.

Divide the remaining wine among 4 dessert plates and place 2 slices of bread soufflés on top. Dust with confectioner's sugar and serve.

Stuffed Almond Apple
with Cranberries

WOLFGANG BIERER, CMPC, AAC, EXECUTIVE CHEF, NESTLE FOODSERVICE USA

Cranberries are a true American favorite—about ninety percent of the world's harvested cranberries are consumed in North America alone. You'll want to try this dessert when the berries are at their best in the early fall season.

MAKES 10 SERVINGS

FOR THE CHOCOLATE CREAM:

5 cups heavy cream, cold

1 cup sugar

1/3 cup cocoa powder

1 tablespoon rum

FOR THE STUFFED APPLES:

10 small apples (Cadey or Granny Smith)

6 cups white wine

juice of 2 lemons

1 cup plus 1 tablespoon sugar

2 cups Chocolate Cream (see recipe)

2 tablespoons rum

5 ounces Toasted Almond Sticks liqueur

1 pound cranberries

1 tablespoon cornstarch

Chocolate shavings to garnish

TO MAKE THE CHOCOLATE CREAM:

In a large dry bowl, using a wire whisk, beat the cream, stopping as soon as it holds soft peaks. In a small bowl, mix together the sugar and the cocoa powder. Fold the sugar/cocoa mixture and the rum into the whipped cream. Fill a pastry bag fitted with a round tip.

TO MAKE THE STUFFED APPLES:

Peel the apples, then core them by digging into the stem end using a melon baller with about a 1-inch diameter; leave the bottom intact.

In a saucepan just large enough to hold the apples in 1 layer, combine 2 cups of the white wine, lemon juice, and all but 1/3 cup of the sugar. Bring to a boil, stirring to dissolve the sugar. Place the apples into the pan, and lower the heat to simmer. Cook, covered until the apples are tender but still firm, about 20 minutes. Transfer the apples to a baking pan or platter and lace with the Almond Sticks. Let cool slightly, then pipe the Chocolate Cream into the center of each apple. Cover and refrigerate.

In a medium saucepan, combine the cranberries with the remaining sugar and white wine. Bring to a boil, lower the heat to simmer, and cook, stirring often, for 5 to 10 minutes. Strain the cranberries from the liquid, returning the liquid to the saucepan and placing the cranberries in a bowl. Whisk the cornstarch into the saucepan, bring the mixture to a boil, and cook, whisking constantly until thickened, 2 to 3 minutes. Pour the sauce into the bowl with the cranberries, and set aside to cool.

To serve, place an apple in the center of a serving plate and surround with the cranberry sauce. Garnish with chocolate shavings.

Apple Custard Tart

STEVE LA COUNT, CEC, AAC, THE COUNTRY CLUB, BROOKLINE, MA

Apples were introduced to America by early settlers in Plymouth, Massachusetts in the early 1600s. Not long after, cider, particularly fermented hard cider, outranked coffee and tea as the most common beverage. There are now more than seven thousand apple varieties, and the average American consumes about forty pounds per year. This apple tart was created to be served with the Lemon Champagne Zabaglione on the following page, although you could serve it with whipped cream or ice cream.

MAKES 8 SERVINGS

One 9-inch tart dough (see page 162-163)

4 large Cortland apples, peeled, cored and cut into
¼-inch thick slices (another variety of baking
apple such as Empire, may be substituted)

⅔ cup sugar

½ teaspoon ground cinnamon

¼ teaspoon allspice

½ lemon, zest grated and juice squeezed

Pinch salt

2 large eggs

1 cup heavy cream

½ cup all-purpose flour

2 tablespoons Calvados, or substitute apple cider

Powdered sugar, for dusting

Preheat the oven to 350°F.

Roll out the tart dough, pressing lightly, from the center out, dusting with flour, as necessary, on and under the dough to prevent sticking. Continue to roll until it is at least 10 inches in diameter and less than ¼-inch thick.

Center the dough in a 9-inch pie plate. Press the dough to the bottom and the sides and trim the dough, leaving a ¼- to ½-inch reserve all the way around. Crimp the dough between two fingers to form a decorative crust. Place a piece of foil wrap on the bottom of the dough and fill with dried beans or pie weights. Prebake the crust, 15 minutes. Set aside to cool on a wire rack. Leave the oven set at 350°F.

In a large bowl, toss the apples, ⅓ cup of the sugar, the cinnamon, allspice, lemon juice and zest, and salt. Set aside, about 20 minutes. Drain the apples and spread them evenly on the prepared pie shell.

To prepare a custard, whisk together the eggs and the remaining ⅓ cup of sugar until pale. Beat in the cream, flour, and the Calvados, if using. When the mixture is well blended, pour it over the apples. Place the pie pan on a baking sheet, and bake in the preheated oven until the custard starts to puff, 25 to 30 minutes. Sprinkle with the powdered sugar and return to the oven until browned, about 10 minutes. Let cool for 20 minutes before eating warm, although it can eaten at room temperature as well. Store any leftovers in the refrigerator.

Lemon Champagne Zabaglione

STEVE LA COUNT, CEC, AAC, THE COUNTRY CLUB, BROOKLINE, MA

Zabaglione (or *sabayon*) is a classic Italian dessert made with sweet Marsala wine. This is a lighter, Americanized version made with champagne or sparkling wine. It is best eaten immediately, spooned over fruit or a simple cake. I created this quick and easy dessert preparation specifically for the Apple Custard Tart on the preceding page; both are best when served warm.

MAKES 6 SERVINGS

4 large eggs

³/₄ cup sugar

1 lemon, juice squeezed and zest grated

¹/₃ cup champagne or American sparkling wine

Add 2 inches of water to the bottom of a double boiler and bring to a boil, then adjust the heat so that it steams. Combine all the ingredients in the top of a double boiler, place it over the bottom, and whisk constantly until the mixture becomes frothy and thick, about 3 minutes. Serve immediately.

Double Chocolate Biscotti

NOBLE MASI, CMB, AAC, CEPC, INSTRUCTOR,
THE CULINARY INSTITUTE OF AMERICA, HYDE PARK, NY

In the late nineteenth and early twentieth centuries, Italians immigrated to America in huge numbers. Many settled in the New York City and Hudson Valley areas. No one can argue that Italian food has become inextricably linked to American cooking, both in restaurants and home kitchens. Indeed, many so-called American classics, like macaroni and cheese, were created by Italians. Biscotti, the Italian twice-baked cookie, has been served well by the American coffee-bar craze seen over the last decade, and has become a part of our food vocabulary.

MAKES ABOUT 4 DOZEN COOKIES

1 cup whole raw almonds

1 cup (2 sticks) unsalted butter,
    at room temperature

3 cups sugar

5 large eggs

$^1/_2$ cup cocoa powder

3$^3/_4$ cups all-purpose flour

1 tablespoon baking powder

1$^1/_4$ cups semisweet chocolate chips

Preheat the oven to 325°F.

Place the almonds in a small baking dish and place in the oven until lightly browned, about 15 minutes. Set aside. Reduce the oven temperature to 300°F.

Using an electric mixer set on medium speed, cream the butter and sugar until fluffy, about 10 minutes. Beat in the eggs, one at a time. Add the cocoa powder. Sift the flour and baking powder into the batter and mix until combined. Fold the almonds and chocolate chips into the dough.

Lightly grease 2 baking sheets with butter and dust with flour, tapping off any excess.

Divide the dough in quarters and shape into 2-inch wide x 1-inch high loafs. Arrange 2 loaves on each pan, at least 4 inches away from each other. Bake, 25 to 30 minutes, until they begin to brown and crack on the top. Remove the pans from the oven and let cool slightly. When they are cool enough to handle, cut into $^1/_2$-inch thick slices, using a serrated knife. Spread the slices on the baking sheet, return the pan to the oven, and bake until they are lightly brown and dry, about 10 minutes.

Tiramisu China Point

BERT P. CUTINO, CEC, AAC, CHAIRMAN OF AAC 1995-1999,
CO-FOUNDER, THE SARDINE FACTORY RESTAURANT, MONTEREY, CA

Tiramisu has become so popular in America, it appears on dessert menus everywhere, Italian or not. When I was growing up and heard the word, I thought it was a Chinese dessert. So I thought why not create a variation on the classic, with won ton crackers instead of the traditional lady fingers? Use the freshest berries, like the ones we get in the nearby valleys, whenever possible.

MAKES 4 SERVINGS

3 large eggs, divided

1/2 cup sugar

1/2 cup Kahlua

2 tablespoons rum

12 ounces marscapone cheese

1 cup espresso

2 tablespoons Sambuca

2 tablespoons powdered sugar

1 teaspoon ground cinnamon

12 each won ton crackers (2-inchs x 2-inches)

1 ounce chocolate shavings

1 cup raspberry sauce (see recipe)

1 cup mixed berries (raspberries, blueberries, and
    strawberries if available)

FOR THE RASPBERRY SAUCE:

1 pound fresh raspberries (can substitute frozen,
    thawed, and drained)

1 cup sugar

In the bowl of a standing mixer or using a hand-held mixer, beat the egg yolks with the sugar until they are pale, 2 to 3 minutes. Add the Kahlua and the rum and mix for a minute, until blended, then add the mascarpone cheese and beat another 2 to 3 minutes. Set aside.

In a separate bowl, whip the egg whites until they form stiff peaks. Fold the egg whites into the mascarpone mixture. Set aside.

In a small bowl, combine the espresso and Sambuca. In another small bowl, mix together the powdered sugar and cinnamon. Transfer the sugar mixture into a small, fine sieve set over a plate.

To serve, place a generous dollop (about $1/4$ cup) of the mascarpone cream onto the center of each serving plate. Dip a wonton cracker into the coffee mixture until mostly saturated but still firm. Dust both sides of the cracker with the sugar/cinnamon mix and place it flatly over the cream on the plate. Repeat this step twice, ending with a dusted won ton cracker, to build a small tower. Sprinkle some shaved chocolate on top and spoon about $1/4$ cup of the raspberry sauce around the base. Sprinkle the mixed berries around the sauce and serve.

TO MAKE THE RASPBERRY SAUCE:

Prepare the raspberry sauce up to a day in advance, combining the raspberries with the sugar in a medium bowl. Puree in a food processor or beat until smooth. Pass the mixture through a fine sieve to remove seeds. Cover and refrigerate until ready to use.

Peach & Rice Timbale with Orange Sauce

ALBERT I. M. IMMING, CMPC, CCE, AAC, CULINARY CONSULTANT,
JOLIET JUNIOR COLLEGE, JOLIET, IL

A timbale is a dish prepared in a mold, usually custard based, although it's usually a technique reserved for savory, not sweet dishes. Peaches are an American favorite, of course, however this recipe represents a melding of cultures, particularly through the use of basmati rice, a staple of Indian cooking.

MAKES 10 SERVINGS

4 gelatin sheets (available from gourmet shops)

3 tablespoons basmati rice

2 cups milk

Grated zest of ½ lemon

1 to 2 drops vanilla extract

1 cup sugar

¼ tablespoon butter

1 large egg yolk

1 cup heavy cream, whipped

1½ pounds ripe peaches

Chocolate shavings for garnish

FOR THE ORANGE SAUCE:

1 cup orange juice

⅔ cup sugar

Grated zest of 2 oranges

2 tablespoons Cointreau

Preheat the oven to 350°F.

Soak the gelatin sheets in 2 cups of cold water for 20 minutes. Meanwhile, heat a small pot of water to a boil, add the rice, and blanch for 2 minutes. Strain.

Place the blanched rice in a casserole with the milk, lemon peel, vanilla, sugar and butter, and bring to a boil on the stovetop. Cover the casserole and transfer to the preheated oven. Stir occasionally, and cook for 20 to 30 minutes. Remove from the oven, remove and discard the lemon peel, and fold in the egg yolk. Let cool.

Bring a very large pot of water to a boil. Carefully add the peaches and cook for just a minute to blanch. Transfer the peaches to a bowl of ice water to cool them down quickly and stop the cooking. Peel the peaches and cube the flesh.

Squeeze the gelatin dry. Put in a small saucepan and melt over low heat, stirring. Fold the melted gelatin into the rice mixture. Fold the whipped cream into the rice mixture, and then fold in about a cup of the peach cubes. Pour the mixture into a ring mold and refrigerate until solid.

When you're ready to serve, prepare the orange sauce. In a saucepan, combine the orange juice, sugar, and orange zest, and bring to a boil. Cook until reduced by a third, 5 to 10 minutes. Remove from the heat and stir in the Cointreau.

Unmold the ring onto a platter. Place the remaining peaches in the center of the ring, and top with the orange sauce.

Linzertorte

MANFRED BAST, CMPC, AAC, RESTAURANT SCHOOL OF PHILADELPHIA, PHILADELPHIA, PA

Linzertorte may be a traditional Austrian dessert, but raspberries are a true American favorite. Oregon's cool spring rains and rich soil support some of the richest growing regions in the world, particularly the Willamette Valley, well known for its caneberries. A caneberry is the term for any of a number of berries that grow on canes, including raspberries, blackberries, boysenberries, and loganberries. From June through September, the Willamette Valley is teaming with caneberries, but this recipe calls for raspberry preserves so that you can make it any time of year.

MAKES 8 SERVINGS

1 cup (2 sticks) unsalted butter, softened

1/2 cup sugar

1 cup ground almonds (use a food processor)

1 teaspoon freshly grated lemon zest

2 hard-boiled large egg yolks, pressed through a sieve

2 teaspoons vanilla extract

1 3/4 cups all-purpose flour

1/8 teaspoon ground cloves

1/4 teaspoon ground cinnamon

Pinch salt

3/4 cup raspberry preserves that have been pressed through a sieve

Beaten egg for egg wash

Preheat the oven to 350°F.

In a mixing bowl, cream together the butter, sugar, ground almonds, zest, and cooked egg yolks. Add the raw egg yolks and vanilla and beat until smooth.

In another bowl, sift together the flour, spices and salt. Work the flour mixture into the creamed mixture to make a smooth dough. Wrap the dough in plastic and chill until firm in the refrigerator.

Remove the dough from the plastic and press into a 10-inch tart ring with a removable bottom. (For a classic preparation, the tart pan should be unfluted.) Press the dough about halfway up the sides of the pan. Spread the preserves evenly over the bottom of the torte.

Use a pastry bag with a plain tip to pipe out the remaining dough over the top of the torte in a lattice pattern and to make a border around the rim. Brush the eggwash over the top of the dough.

Bake the torte for about 25 minutes, or until the pastry is golden brown. Unmold from the pan and serve.

Open-Face Apple Cake

MANFRED BAST, CMPC, AAC, RESTAURANT SCHOOL OF PHILADELPHIA, PHILADELPHIA, PA

Try this dessert if you love apple pie, but want to surprise your family and friends with something a bit different. Red Rome apples, originally from Ohio, but now widely grown in New York State as well, are ideally suited to this dish, but the commonly available McIntosh will be just as delicious.

MAKES 8 SERVINGS

2 cups all-purpose flour

$^1/_3$ cup plus $^1/_2$ cup sugar

Grated zest of 1 lemon

10 tablespoons unsalted butter

1 large egg

1 large egg yolk

$^1/_8$ teaspoon salt

$^3/_4$ tablespoon white vinegar

$^3/_4$ tablespoon cold water

4 tart apples

$^1/_2$ cup finely chopped walnuts

$^1/_2$ cup golden raisins

2 teaspoons cinnamon

4 tablespoons unsalted butter, melted

1 beaten large egg for egg wash

Confectioner's sugar for dusting

In a large mixing bowl, stir together the flour, $^1/_3$ cup of the sugar and the lemon rind. Using a pastry blender or two butter knives, cut in the butter until the dough resembles a coarse meal.

In another bowl, combine the egg, egg yolk, vinegar, water and salt. Make a well in the flour-butter mixture and add the wet ingredients. Using a fork, slowly blend the wet ingredients into the dough. Press the dough into a rectangle about 1 inch thick and chill until firm.

To prepare the apples, peel them and cut into $^1/_8$-inch-thick slices. Cover and refrigerate to prevent browning.

Preheat the oven to 350°F.

Roll the chilled dough into a rectangle 16 inches long by 12 inches wide. Transfer the dough to a parchment-lined half-sized sheet pan. Cover the dough with a lengthwise strip of apple slices, leaving a 2-inch margin all around. Scatter two-thirds of the chopped walnuts over the apples. Scatter half the raisins over the apples too.

In a small bowl, combine the remaining $^1/_2$ cup of sugar and the cinnamon, and dust half of the mixture over the apples. Cover with another layer of apple slices and scatter the remaining nuts and raisins over the top. Sprinkle the top with the remaining sugar-cinnamon mixture.

Fold the short edges of the dough up, then the long edges. Brush the egg wash on the border strips. Spoon the melted butter over the filling. Bake in the oven for 35 to 45 minutes, until the crust is golden. Cool to room temperature before serving. Cut the pastry into 1-inch slices and dust with confectioner's sugar.

Spring Strawberry Rhubarb Sorbet

BARBARA SANDERS, MS, CCE, AAC, CULINARY INSTRUCTOR/CONSULTANT, MONROE, NH

Russian trappers established rhubarb in the area that is now Alaska early in the seventeenth century. By the middle of the nineteenth century, it was a popular ingredient in the New England states, filling baked goods and being pressed into wine. Today, rhubarb marks the arrival of spring in the East. This recipe is the base for frozen sorbet, but other ideas might include serving it as a soup, topped with a dollop of sour cream; adding a sparkling cider to make a punch; or reducing it until syrupy and using it as a sauce for game or chocolate desserts. Strawberry rhubarb is a specific variety. You can use ordinary rhubarb, but the color of the sorbet will be less vivid.

MAKES 10 SERVINGS

3 stalks strawberry rhubarb, finely chopped

1 quart apple cider

$^1/_2$ apple, peeled, cored, and chopped

$^1/_2$-inch piece fresh ginger, peeled and minced

1 star anise

$^1/_2$ cup maple syrup

1 cup drained and chopped canned beets

1 cinnamon stick

Sliced strawberries and fresh mint leaves
   for garnish, optional

Combine all the ingredients except for the strawberries and the mint in a medium, nonreactive saucepan and place over high heat. Bring to a boil, reduce the heat, and simmer 30 minutes. Set aside to steep for 1 hour. Strain the liquid (to maintain a vibrant color do not press the solids), and transfer to a 2-quart ice cream maker. Discard the solids. Prepare the sorbet following the manufacturer's instructions. Serve garnished with a fresh strawberry slice and a mint leaf, if desired.

Index

FRITZ SONNENSCHMIDT, Certified Master Chef, is the Culinary Dean at the Culinary Institute of America in Hyde Park, New York, the host of the PBS show *Cooking Secrets of the CIA,* and the current Chair of the American Academy of Chefs.

DENNIS GOTTLIEB is a New York-based food photographer who has collaborated on many cookbook projects. He lives in New Jersey with his wife and son.